# SOLAR
## SUCCESS PRINCIPLES
How to Make a **Difference** and a **Fortune**
in the **Green Economy**

# KEITH CRONIN

Published by: SunHedge LLC

ISBN 13: 978-0-9829471-0-4

Cover and Interior Formatting: Streetlight Graphics
Editor: Renee Ergazos

Printed and Bound in the United States of America

*This book is dedicated to my Dad, Joseph Cronin. He always told me to follow my passion and to serve others. His encouragement was a constant source to learn from and he will never be forgotten. My gratitude for his wisdom, teaching, and philosophy has helped shape who I am today.*

# TABLE OF CONTENTS

# ACKNOWLEDGEMENTS

For those that know me, my constant echoing of "every day is a gift" follows them and reminds me of how appreciative I am to awaken every day and transcend the meaning I give to the day. My list of acknowledgements could be a book unto itself, but I will do my best to identify the people responsible for their influence on me. I apologize in advance for missing anyone, as this is not an exhaustive list.

This book is dedicated to my father, Joseph Cronin. Due to an illness, he checked out way too soon, but I always feel he is around me, encouraging me! It was he who taught me to follow my dreams and encouraged all of the people he came in contact with. He has left a positive impression for what is possible with a little imagination and hard work. I owe him immensely for instilling in me a strong work ethic early in my life and revealing our human capacity to give, which has influenced my success in many immeasurable ways. He also encouraged me to make time each week to have something to look forward to, like a group activity or a sport with others, as this is also an intrinsic catalyst for doing things not just for yourself, but your extended tribe! We all love you and miss you.

Elizabeth, my mom, you also have been a guiding light of encouragement and coaching too! Your balanced approach to any dilemma is always a source of enlightenment when we speak and I always look forward to your perspective. You, like Dad, are also a giver to the community and always stop to help others in need. Your desire to do outreach work and contribute are a constant reminder and a well that I drink from often. Love you too mom!

My stepparents also deserve a lot of gratitude for enduring my presence as they helped in my evolution. To my sisters, half-sister, stepsisters, and stepbrothers (a.k.a. the family forest) thanks for the feedback and perspective. Layers of aunts and uncles giving of themselves to our Brady Bunch environment in the early years also provided me with a balanced approach to life.

My daughter Claire, I am blessed to have you in my orbit and I truly love being your father! Watching you grow and make new distinctions and guiding you when you need help inspires me. I love you very much!

To my close friends back east; it seems I have so many connections, but you know who you are!

Tony Maciorski, he was my inspiration for solar and was the catalyst to come to Hawaii to change the world—Mahalo!

My business mentor Frank Blau, the man with a mission to teach number crunching to anyone that would be receptive and who wanted to embrace a new way of thinking for contractors. He revolutionized how thousands of tradespeople think and look at business and has undoubtedly influenced thousands more outside of the building trades. If you don't have any business mentors, go now and seek them out, as they want to help you.

Jim Hamilton and Steve Schneider are fantastic business gurus who helped when I needed it most by answering my endless stream of questions and rewiring my brain.

Perry and Marilyn Hodges, I can't believe you never blocked my calls; thank you for encouraging me and being there to provide me with my awakening.

My friends Ron Dorris, Tom Shuster, and Jackie Pankraz, thanks for supporting my goals and answering my plethora of questions and being great friends. Even though we are far away in different time zones, you are my personal board of directors!

Steve Allen, for the introduction into new and visionary ways to run a successful company!

Joe and Diane Harding—the "hanai" family in Hawai'i—they took me into their world when I established a beach head in Hawai'i and nurtured me and were always there to help me with whatever I needed. You personify *aloha* and why Hawaii is special. Mahalo!

Randall Murphy, a sales guru when it comes to assisted buying. You've been a great sounding board!

Charlene Sunada, "nurse able." A woman that was always able to help me with anything, anytime. Next time you see or meet a nurse, give one a big hug of thanks and gratitude as it's hard to fully understand what they go through every day for us!

I have so many friends in Hawaii that I want to say thank you to, but you know me and know I'd want to limit the amount of deforesting that will occur in the printing of this book.

Jigar Shah and Brian Robertson, from the early days at Sun Edison when their idea had just taken root, they are both visionaries who have become my great friends. Jigar had an amazing idea that has been copied across the globe: bringing solar to the masses. Brian was there from the beginning to assist him, with his incredible ability to make complicated things easy. Brian has left all of us recently, further inspiring those who had the pleasure to know him to make a difference in the world. Thanks for the big break and believing in me. You can't even imagine how the experience has influenced me, and I will always be grateful!

Marco Mangelsdorf, like me, believed in starting a solar business in Hawaii, when it wasn't popular or an important business. Thank you for being a source of encouragement and continuing to see what is possible in a business that can be full of uncertainty.

My gratitude goes to the solar pioneers Cully Judd and Rick Reed of Inter Island Solar Supply, Jeff Wolfe, David Katz, Richard Perez, and a whole lot more, and to the folks at SEIA, RMI, IREC, ASES, and all the acronym entities that I missed.

Our elected officials and the legislative process: Tirelessly these people give of themselves and work for us. They, by far, help shape the policy decisions that affect all of us. Early on, it was patently clear to me that if I wanted to see change, I needed to be part of it. Learning about how our democracy works via investing time in the legislative process, either crafting bills and or testifying on them, is a right I never took for granted. I encourage you to do the same because your voice needs to be heard.

Renee Ergazos has been my editor extraordinaire on this book. Keeping me focused, giving my voice clarity, and cutting through the dense jungle of my mind's words has been a source of encouragement and delight. You've made me a much better author than I would have been without you. Without your constant positive feedback and surgical skills, which any author needs when getting out their message via ink on paper, this book would not have been possible. Gratitude is an understatement.

Glendon Haddix of Streetlight Graphics is the architect behind the interior and exterior of this book. Your talent and desire to serve is very much appreciated.

There are so many people that have become friends over the years that I want to acknowledge, yet I know some of them desire to remain anonymous. I respect you for being the silent heros in our global community. The historical figures that I'd seek to list would be a book unto itself.

A future acknowledgment to those that get inspired with their dreams and plans: take action towards a goal and stay focused. If I can do it, so can you. Whether it's in a green business or you have found a way to help the people in your community, I encourage you to be decisive and contribute and make the world a better place.

# INTRODUCTION

Today, solar has become the preeminent way of creating energy and is revolutionizing how we use energy across the globe. From Hawaii to Italy or Canada to Japan, solar has captured the imagination of homeowners, businesses, governments, and entrepreneurs. There will be millions to be made in this business while simultaneously allowing many people and businesses to make a difference both locally and globally in creating indigenous energy and using it on site.

Solar energy is creating jobs in our new green economy today, where a lot of companies are struggling to make money and to find jobs. The competition is fierce as countries, states, and provinces across the world are opening up to the solar marketplace and seeing hundreds of competitors.

Solar companies desire viability and their drive to take market share is unprecedented. In consulting, what I've found is that a lot of companies are completely focused on making more sales and forgo making any profits in the hopes that they can eventually crush their competitors. One of the challenges with this approach is that the solar industry is plagued with gross margins that are already low to begin with, and these margins seem to follow the same trajectory as the construction industry of low profitability and high risk. When a company focuses on making more sales, it is creating challenges for itself, from having enough working capital, to being able to pay their vendors, pay their employees, and paying their taxes. They also struggle to support and service existing customers' needs as the company craves the allure of new customers as their salvation for profitability.

This book was written because I heard a calling to amalgamate information and trends happening globally and to offer a perspective of where we are and where we are going in the solar industry. Whether you provide residential solar services or are one of the large national solar service providers to hedge funds and portfolio managers at large lending institutions, this was written for you. If you're a manufacturer of products that are utilized in the solar industry—solar panels, inverters, balance of system components, monitoring, etc.—you will be served by the content as well.

Knowing the mindset of small to large solar integration companies is pivotal to knowing the trends of the industry. Understanding where things are going and how you can partner with the industry to see its success, whether it's on grid solar projects or you decide to explore deploying solar in a developing nation, the principles outlined in this book will be the seeds of your success.

While there have been many books written about solar and business, none combine the foundational principles of each. So this crucible happened as a result of feedback from the industry and clients across the globe as well as so many newcomers wanting to also make a difference and add value to their markets and become leaders in their towns, cities and provinces.

As the global economy has been teetering for some time, people's desire to go back to work and potentially apply their existing skills and knowledge in the solar space has been unprecedented. Investment bankers to electricians are all seeking work in this blossoming industry.

Energy, by far is the largest industry in the world and with the increase in population, will only bring more demand for more energy. The question is, what will be the source and who will finance, engineer, install, and maintain it? Driving down the price of solar is what everyone wants to see, especially when we look at the subsidized structure of solar and we all want the training wheels to come off sooner rather than later.

The principles in this book aren't just about solar, but for me, solar is going to be my example for you. If you're in any business that has employees and you sell your time (we have become a service industry in the USA) and maybe a widget (materials) or two, the principles inside this book will help you get focused, make a difference, add value, and allow you to live the life you've always dreamed.

I will outline the simple tools in this book to help you understand what it takes keep the lights on in your company each day, each week, and each month. My metaphor is to illustrate that you'll know what your daily, weekly, and monthly costs are and work backwards from there to develop the framework for success at your organization.

Take the journey with me in this book. The story doesn't stop at the last page; I've included some free resources to accompany this book to assist you further in reaching your goals.

# CHAPTER ONE

# SOLAR TODAY: TRENDS AND PATTERNS

In the last 2 years there has been explosive growth across the globe from Germany to Hawaii and all points in between. We've seen solar panel manufacturer capacity increase to a point where there is actually overcapacity in the marketplace today. This would've been unheard of only 4 years ago when you had to pay a premium for solar modules, and panel rationing was happening at the manufacturer level to their distribution partners.

The advent of micro-inverter technology has streamlined many of the engineering processes involved in the design and installation of photovoltaic systems. This has been clearly seen on the urban solar market, most specifically in the residential sector. It has simplified solar installations and added a level of measurable performance accountability on each individual solar panel that the industry was sorely lacking for decades. Clean AC power coming off the roof is also relatively new for an industry that will attract more manufacturers and innovation.

The opportunity to consider purchasing a photovoltaic system out right with cash used to be the only option available, but now a solar system can be leased like leasing a car, or customers can even enter into a power purchase agreement, which essentially is like buying a mortgage over 20 years to cover the cost of equipment that encompasses a solar system. Again, I point to Jigar Shah and Sun Edison for making this idea mainstream and the defacto way that solar is going to be deployed in the future.

Technical training and widespread adoption from homeowners to businesses has made the solar industry a household name. There is a training class happening every day in some city near you to jump start your career in solar or get you additional training to further hone your skills. States seem to be opening up every month with new incentive programs aimed at solar adoption by homeowners and businesses. States like Texas, which have been predominantly driven by fossil fuels, have finally implemented solar energy incentive programs and are harnessing the power of the sun.

# WHAT HAS REALLY CHANGED IN THE SOLAR INDUSTRY?

For one, the competition and how to overcome the market saturation has evolved as people and businesses are descending into areas from across the globe. Solar businesses are eager to acquire customers and buy projects either already built or in someone's pipeline of projects on the cusp of being developed. When the world financial crisis hit, many people lost their jobs and this really impacted all of us, specifically when one of the main drivers in our economy, which is construction, came to a screeching halt. This has become the perfect storm for the solar industry, as now we've been able to tap into a pool of skilled tradespeople who want to immerse themselves in a new field of construction and utilize their existing skills to improve the best practices of an emerging industry.

Many of the people that used to be building homes, putting roofs on homes, and wiring homes now have found employment in the solar industry. Opportunities in solar has also stretched outside of the residential marketplace and into the commercial and industrial sectors as well. Traditional contracting entities have decided solar has become a growth industry not just in their location but by giving them the impetus to be able to expand globally.

# WE NEED TO TALK ABOUT THE BAD NEWS AS WELL

The data has spoken. While the average selling price for the cost per watt for installing solar has gone down, so have gross margins. Add in the fact that governments across the globe have been inconsistent in public policy as it relates to the incentives that are currently in the marketplace.

This has fueled boom and bust cycles from Germany to California. The incentives either become too rich, feeding large organizations rolling into a local solar program's feed in tariff queue and scooping up whatever is in the program queue, or the incentives haven't gotten many people interested in going solar in certain markets and therefore limited the interest of solar developers. We've mostly seen the former happen from Spain to Canada. It's very challenging for utilities and local governments to establish a standard framework and policy decisions to avoid the boom and bust cycles associated with incentive programs. There is a limited economic resource base, and local utilities are mostly unable to accept and effectively manage all of the nonfirm energy generated by the solar resources.

This has caused a ripple in middle- to larger-sized solar companies that believed they were well-established, only to find out that somebody operating out of their garage has beat them on price, because large organizations have much higher overheads than the mom-and-pop shops. The barriers to entering into the solar business are very low, so it is easy to get into this industry with little money. The smaller businesses are agile and often woven into the community. When consumers look at the price of a solar system for their home, as an example, the difference in price from a larger solar integration company to the mom-and-pop shops often causes them to receive multiple quotes and creates a stampede towards being the lowest cost provider in the area, further fueling a race to the bottom mindset.

Another challenge that is encountered is that due to the heavy competition in the solar industry, there are very high customer acquisition costs. In the marketplace today, our customer acquisition costs range from $500 upwards of $2,000 per new residential customer. If the solar industry were a very high-margin business then we shouldn't be concerned, unfortunately it is not. This alone should be a cause of concern for you, as the money has to come from somewhere: either your pocket or your customers. In a crowded marketplace, lowering this cost is crucial.

An outdated sales compensation plan can also be detrimental to a company. I do believe that people in sales or business development should be compensated well, but today's industry has very little shared responsibility or shared accountability between sales and operations. That needs to change for the companies to become profitable and be in it for the long-haul as some sales compensation plans have the salespeople making more money than the company, while assuming little to no risk.

As you can see, a new approach is needed. For your company to not just survive, but thrive in the marketplace today, you need to adjust your approach. This can come in many forms such as partnering with other building trades, financial institutions, and vendors so you can maintain adequate cash flow and retained earnings, or you will be a commodity with a very short shelf life.

# WHO WINS AND WHO LOSES IN THIS NEW WORLD?

How is solar sold, deployed, serviced, and ultimately owned? The level of visibility in the marketplace today has created an environment where businesses and homeowners solicit many solar companies to provide them bids for projects. The companies that will win will have to adapt and adopt more streamlined business models in order to make money and serve their customers. The days of making high gross margins have come to an end.

With this increased pressure to stay out of the commodity business, what are you to do? Do you know who your customers are? Do you know which customers aren't really your customers? Is your company still working on three part OCR forms? Have you made your operations and sales process web-based?

If you read the above paragraph and answered no to any of the questions, you might have some challenges moving forward with your business. Other companies today are streamlining their operations, creating shared responsibility between sales and operations, and rewarding results in excellence versus the old days of just paying a commission and praying you can get the job done for what you quoted your customer for.

## SO WHY IS THIS?

It really comes down to the customer and what their needs are versus you telling them what they think they need, as again, they are getting multiple bids and are using the Internet as a resource prior to make a decision on who to do business with. The analogy is similar to buying a car today. You go on the Internet to a car dealer's website and do the research prior to making a decision. The same rules for solar have emerged and are only going to continue. Customers are using social media and talking to their friends, family, and coworkers about their experience with your company and the results they've had with you. Even the large solar farms that are being built have all of this information public, and decision-makers for those projects are accessible today and will share their experiences with others. What do you want them to say about you?

## HOW DID I FIGURE ALL OF THIS OUT?

After my company was acquired by Sun Edison and I finished my tenure with the company, many new and existing solar companies contacted me and asked for help. Three weeks after my Sun Edison exit, I still wanted to serve others and I realized there was a demand for assistance in a host of areas in the solar business, so I started my consulting practice.

Being invited into other businesses gave me the visibility to understand what their challenges were and to offer them the solutions that I used in my own company prior to the acquisition. I could also implement things I learned in the 10 years prior to the acquisition about solar and business. It never ceased to amaze me that when I was invited into a company and asked a business owner what was their biggest frustration, what I would hear. There was a resounding consistent theme with most of them as it related to sales, operations, customer service, and the usual internal challenges associated with the hyper growth being experienced by the solar industry.

The suggestions in this book can be applied to many businesses that offer services bundled with products where the service is selling time. This falls under any construction-related activity but also expands beyond construction into other types of businesses that sell their time plus a percentage of their products to represent the other percentage of the pie chart.

We are in a service economy in the United States, so this is applicable to so many small businesses and this book will give you the tools and strategies to keep you on track and help you avoid the pitfalls.

Quite often when I meet people at a new company and they ask for some consulting or advice, I find similar trends at companies across the country. When people believe that they are all alone and they are the only ones going through their situation they can be surprised to learn that they are normal. In some ways it is quite the opposite, as the DNA of problems exists in every company but the ones that are successful recognize the gap in their shortcomings and decide to be proactive and do something about it. This is the difference between successful companies and ones that just get by.

The tools, information, and knowledge in this book will allow you, if applied, to take your business to the next level. What I mean by the next level is not always in monetary terms.

Whether it's improving your customer service, your sales and operations, accountability, lowering your customer acquisition costs, or sharing the success metrics in your organization, I will show you a road map. You can have a company that is not only legendary, but also has the framework so if you decide that you would like to pursue something else in your life, you can by choice and not by force. We will show you how to develop a clear and defined exit strategy as well as a succession planning map for the future for when, and not if, you can hand the torch off to the people, person, or company of your choosing.

Let's create a compelling future for you, your family, your company, and your community.

# CHAPTER TWO

# HOW I DID IT

In the early days of starting my company, I believed that I could do it all. I watched my last boss do it, so I thought, how hard could it be? The realization hits hard, when I recognized being an entrepreneur required me to work 24/7/365 just to get the company off the ground and stabilized. Unless you are a well-funded startup, most businesses, like mine, start off bootstrapped.

Starting in the garage is never easy, but as I look back, it was very rewarding as I now appreciate the devotion, dedication, and focus needed to bring my ideas to life and see them in action. I moved to Hawaii from the East Coast and did not know anyone when I arrived. I ambitiously decided to start a solar company in 1998, with the core philosophy of making a difference and serving the community.

Solar photovoltaic systems were not very well adopted in 1998 due to the exorbitant cost of solar modules, so we needed to offer other services in order to grow the business at the time. In those early years we offered other services as an electrical contracting company. We worked for the Department of Defense, the city and county, commercial, retail, and residential houses with a simple mantra: anywhere we could serve our community, we would by offering our services in the energy field via energy efficiency, education, and electrical services, all to build relationships.

In 1999 through 2004 there was a boom in construction in Hawaii and it was directly related to the dot-com growth. Many people became instant millionaires as a result of getting stock options, and they came from New York to California and across the globe. A steady stream of instant millionaires was eager to have Hawaii their new home or their second or third homes.

While this was an exciting time to be in construction or development it was also a challenging time as many businesses would just grab the work and couldn't say no. They were caught up in the euphoria of the new construction boom and had an endless line of clients eager to build anything at any price.

In the beginning of my company's existence, we were quickly doing hundreds of thousands of dollars' worth of work each month yet we would not be paid in a timely way for our services. How naïve, yet enthusiastic I was about the possibility of being in business and serving others. It's far from simple, especially without a plan and the systems to assist you in dealing with the daily repetitive tasks that take away from building a business and a brand. As I look back, the excitement and struggle shaped who I am today. However, if I had some of the resources I have today, I could have reached my goals sooner with a lot less struggle and pain.

When I started out, I wore lots of different hats and assumed many different roles, which is where I truly cultivated gratitude. Most of the general contractors were originally carpenters and, in general, had very little business experience, but they could build something spectacular. Managing cash flow and a workforce or managing projects was not always their best attribute or something we enjoyed doing. This caused a lot of dissatisfaction for me, my team, and my vision of the future. Something needed to change, and it was me! I decided to really look in the mirror and acknowledge to myself that I needed some business training, and I needed to figure another way to directly connect with consumers and limit being the middleman all the time.

I found a best-practice group that really taught me about crunching numbers and not just about being profitable but truly helping consumers by giving them what they *needed* versus what we thought they *wanted*. I became cognizant of the things that many people who jump into business first and wonder what happened second are not aware of. I knew what it took keep the lights on every day as I had a grip on our overhead costs and a real budget we could work from. We communicated this vision; We shared with our whole company how our company operated and how the money worked and how it impacted them if we were not going to follow an effective plan and strategy. Our employees knew what was expected of them and our customers knew what to expect from us. This caused us to lose some staff but find others who shared our values and vision. Our customers liked the added level of attention and customer service, which was uncharacteristic of companies like ours, and we were told this was something they not only liked but felt compelled to share with others.

I took an interest in the financial aspects of the business, because I felt it was necessary in order to survive in the early days of my business, and I enjoyed math and seeing the difference between revenue and actual profits. Usually in business, the allure of more revenue trumps retained earnings, but it was clear to me that I'd rather have less revenue and more profits if I was going to serve more people effectively.

As I started to crunch the numbers each week, I learned that working as a subcontractor, more money would go out, than come in. As I started dissecting what was going on, I determined that many large organizations that we worked with would leverage our money by building spec homes and doing other things with the resources that were accounts payable to them. It was at this time that I was rather disappointed and frustrated being in business, as I felt that I would be a slave to this lifestyle until I chose to retire.

One fateful day I ran into a friend of mine and I asked him, "How do you get paid in a timely way when you are a subcontractor?" He replied, "I don't know because I am never a subcontractor." He shared with me some business principles that caused me to reevaluate what I was doing with my business and to look at other ways to serve the public and to have better control over the management of my business. I realized I needed to understand business better and focus more on the metrics and less on the technical aspects of the electrical contracting field, which I was already confident, trained, and familiar with. The commitment I made to learning more about business, as I look back in time, was the best decision I ever made in the allocation of my time, and the results spoke for themselves.

Fast forward to 2006-2007 when I was approached by a friend of mine named Jigar Shah, who founded a company called Sun Edison. The company was in hyper growth mode and had started to scale the company. They asked me if I'd like to join their "conga line," and through negotiations, numerous term sheets, and a final agreement, my company was acquired in August 2007.

I became surrounded by people from all over the globe that were phenomenal in business and in their respective disciplines. They were attracting talent from a host of industries and the experience was a once in a lifetime opportunity to further my education and global relationships. Having companies like Goldman Sachs on our board exposed me to insight and opportunities that wouldn't have been possible had I not made the decision to sell my company and be part of a growing global organization that was revolutionizing how solar was financed and delivered.

For many people in business, like me, it takes a point of severe frustration to seek out the knowledge that is needed to propel a company and prepare it for a suitor. Our country is founded upon entrepreneurs, just like yourself, that want to strike out on their own. Now is your time! For the readers that have found this book outside the United States, the principles apply to you as well, as business and math are universal.

One of the most important things I learned through the process of growing a successful company is that it's not always about the money. It perhaps seems unusual for me to say that in a business-oriented book, but I honestly believe it's about what you become in the process and how many people you can serve and ultimately make a positive impact on.

# CHAPTER THREE

# THE ART AND SCIENCE OF BUDGETING

For many new and existing business owners, budgeting is about as exciting as getting four root canals done at the same time. You know it's necessary and you've waited too long to take care of your business, but the pain is too great to endure.

When I speak to businesses, whether it is a small company of five people or more than 100 people in an organization, most of them don't have a budget for the company or do any strategic planning because their days are stuffed with daily tactical maneuvering to just get through the day. Most of the people don't know what the overhead is as a percentage of sales or the job cost of each and every project. They don't know how they did on a job or how they're doing or what went right or wrong. Inertia is carrying them to their destination rather than allowing some basic math and reasoning to propel them.

Big companies and small are equally as guilty in this, as they count on the sales team to create enough cash flow to keep the charade going on. The challenge with this approach is that in the early stage of a company it is not so severe, but like any habit that becomes neglected over time, it atrophies like a muscle that receives no exercise.

And how does this happen? Quite simply, many small businesses do excellent work. In doing excellent work, they get rewarded with referrals and more business. This often requires them to hire more people, yet they forget to allocate some basic processes, like knowing how many hours the new employee is going to be productive over the course of their employment. This usually falls under the auspice of field or operations people. Clients are always in disbelief as to how far off they are in calculating their overhead or labor costs are and how this is impacting their profitability and market share. This also impacts their ability to recruit top talented people and makes them wonder why people are leaving their organization.

Why does this happen? Quite often it stems from our lack of exposure to creating a budget in the first place. Since we are speaking about the solar industry let's look at the background of a typical solar contractor. But you need to know that this affects many businesses: dentists, doctors, attorneys, and beyond. Most business professionals were educated in a specific discipline, but do you think the attorney focused on tort law or business classes? Most professionals running their own business never took a business class and their support staff most likely did not also. Our education system was not designed to show people the basics, whether it be a budget, a business plan, a sales and marketing plan, or how to put it all together.

Most people that I know who enter the solar integrator space as a career come from the building trades background. This is relatively easy to research and understand, as it's a natural extension of what they already do. Typically, most people that are brought up in this environment are taught a lot about technical aspects of how to do something.

Think about an electrician as an example. When I was just starting out I was fortunate enough to go through an apprenticeship training program. Most electricians are exposed to 5 years of education at a minimum. They get to learn all about the electrical code, standards, safety, and other physically related activities that are associated to the installation of products that relate to the type of work that electricians do. The same can be said for carpenters, roofers, and other trades people who are now employed in the solar business.

But if you look at the anatomy of the curriculum, anything related to business is absent. And why is this? Quite simply, apprenticeship training programs are designed to churn out worker bees. Their intent is to build a workforce and not business people. Sure there might be some classes for project management for people elevating to a higher position in a company, but in general this is more of a planning class and does not teach much about how to run and maintain your business. This is also common in the engineering field. Unless you've taken electives in school outside of your normal vocation, business training is usually nonexistent.

# CHAPTER FOUR

# HOW MANY HOURS CAN YOU SELL

How many hours in a calendar year do you believe you can sell? Let me give you some guidelines to help you understand what I see as a continuous challenge for businesses that sell their time and sometimes sell products with their time. Some will call this *time and material billing* and some will meld the two to provide a lump sum for their services. Personally, I like the lump sum method, as long as the scope of work is concise.

Back to the question as many people gloss over this guiding principle: How many hours can you sell? First you need to determine how many hours *are there* to sell? Let us keep the math real simple and say there are 52 weeks in a year and 40 hours in a week: *52 x 40 = 2080* hours. This is if you work every day of every week throughout the year. But you need to subtract time for vacations, holidays, and sick days. Yes, you can work on the weekends and work late into the evenings, but my point is that we all have the same amount of hours regardless of who we are. How we decide to work and how we leverage our time is entirely up to us.

Let's look at the math again. If you want to have a life outside of work to do the things that you love, like spending time with family, friends, hobbies, or whatever else you enjoy doing, you cannot work 2080 hours a year. This holds true for the employees that you are going to be hiring as well. Accept the simple axiom that your employees will also have vacations, sick days, and time off for other things like training, education, personal development time, etc.

Before you hire your first employee, you are going to be employee number one. You will do all the work and all the activities associated with your solar business. You will most likely do it all, from CEO to bookkeeping, unless you have a spouse or family member who is going to assist you. Based upon this premise, how many hours do you believe you can sell? When I say *sell,* I mean figure how many hours you can be out in front of your customers, being productive.

Tasks like installing solar panels and performing all the associated activities surrounding those installs are characterized as productive activities that you can charge your time for. People don't want to pay for the time you spend shopping multiple vendors. If you are the sole employee, my estimate is you will only be able to sell your time for approximately 1,000 hours in a calendar year. This might come as a surprise to you, but if you start tracking your time in regards to the activities that you do every day you'll start to see a pattern.

Some refer to this as *billable time* versus *unbillable time* as well. Whether you need to spend time doing paperwork, creating estimates, driving to and from a project site, or procuring materials, the lists can get quite long for the activities you really don't get paid for. It is easy to see how time can be eroded away in a 24-hour day and, in a bigger picture, over the calendar year.

So, what are you going to sell your time for? If we use the 1000 hours in a year as an example above, how much do you want to charge for your time? You can see why when you call a local attorney and they tell you it's going to be $200 an hour or more for their time, why this is. An attorney is a good example of someone in an industry that sells only its labor. Most attorneys whom I know try hard to bill out 1,600 hours a year, but they are at the office 10 to 12 hours a day because they know they cannot bill for all of their time.

In the solar business you can make money on materials, but as you dive into this book you'll see that I'm a strong advocate of knowing your numbers first. You can always make money on materials, but wouldn't it be better to do the math and work backwards and figure out your baseline assumptions first on your labor costs? In a competitive bidding environment you need to know if you can meet the price of the competitor or if you need to walk from an opportunity.

You can decide what you want to charge for your time and then multiply that by the man-hours that you can sell in a calendar year to determine what your approximate yearly gross salary is going to be. When you start keeping score you might find that you actually sell less than 1,000 hours, which could be a bit of a surprise to you and your CPA when they do your taxes. Wouldn't it be better for you to track your time and know your approximate salary prior to April 15th?

Remember: You cannot manage what you cannot measure. Make it a daily habit to track your activities and keep good records and you'll thank yourself many years into the future. If you look at sports, they consistently track all scores and they measure their performance, so they know how their doing and what to improve upon.

If you are just thinking about starting your own business and you have a lot of work and it's more that you can handle, now you're ready to hire your first employee. If you're already in business, you might want to hire many more employees, but you need to get this budgeting and planning thing in order, once and for all.

Based upon the earlier discussion from above, how many hours of their time do you think your employees are able to sell? How productive are the folks going to be in the field? If you have more work than people, they'll be busy all day long. But the bigger question is, what will they be busy doing? Will they be doing productive things, like installations, or will they be spending time doing other unproductive things, like going to get materials and tasks you can't really bill for?

I'd like to go back to the math for a second, as it relates to the new and existing employees that work in the field installing solar at your company. How productive are they going to be? You need to determine how many productive hours they are going to perform billable tasks. In general, from my statistical research and constant years of tracking at our company, the general rule of thumb is in an 8-hour day, the field people will be productive approximately 75% to 80% of the time, or about 6 hours in a day.

Before we chunk down how we got to these numbers, let's start with a budget for your company and then drill down to the productivity of your field team in a subsequent chapter.

# CHAPTER FIVE

# EXAMPLE BUDGET

There are a plethora of items and categories that go into developing a budget for your company. These categories apply to almost all businesses that sell time, labor, materials, or products. Most service-based businesses in the world blend labor and some materials, or they sell a widget as a package. It doesn't matter if you make refrigerators or install solar.

If you have accounting software, you can usually find many of these costs as line items in a dollar amount and as a percentage. You probably have an accountant or bookkeeper that can pull all of this together for you as well. Part of my success has been embracing the numbers and knowing what I've come to call "my daily nut." How much do I need to "crack" each day in order to feed everyone: the staff (direct costs), the overhead (indirect costs), revenue numbers. I am essentially determining the level of productivity needed based upon some simple metrics that we use to effectively manage our businesses.

This exercise, while not as exciting as selling solar, installing solar, or financing solar is essential for you to know. Companies that hone in on knowing these fundamentals, like understanding their overhead and direct costs, will pay dividends way into the future. It will allow you to run your company rather than the company running you. Take the time, roll up your sleeves, and embrace the numbers. It will either be sobering or exhilarating or both in some instances. Decide when you're done where the money is going to come from: you (the business owner) and your company, or the customer.

There is also a sample of this on our website to compare notes with as a guide, but remember that your numbers will be different from everyone that you might know because each company's structure is a little different. See the references in the back of the book for links to the information.

| Overhead Category #1 —Salaries | # of people | Cost |
|---|---|---|
| Owner's Salary | | |
| Supervisors | | |
| Managers | | |
| Other Field Help | | |
| Bookkeeping | | |
| Accounting | | |
| Customer Service Reps | | |
| Dispatching | | |
| Warehouse | | |
| Other Office Help | | |
| Helpers | | |
| Other Nonfield Compensation | | |
| Sales | | |
| **Sub-Total** | | |
| FICA Taxes- 6.2% | | |
| Medicare Taxes- 1.45 % | | |
| State Unemployment Taxes- 2.0% | | |
| Federal Unemployment Taxes- .012% | | |
| Other Payroll Taxes-depends upon location | | |
| Health Insurance $_____ per employee | | |
| Medical Reimbursement Plan-depends upon location | | |
| Life, Disability & Other Employee Insurance | | |
| Other Employee Benefits- Perks, Gym Membership, etc. | | |
| Retirement Plan Contributions | | |
| **Total Overhead Salaries and Benefits** | | |

| Overhead Category #2:<br>Advertising and Customer Service | Cost |
|---|---|
| **Advertising Total** or *Use Subcategories Below* | |
| Yellow Pages | |
| TV | |
| Radio | |
| Newspaper | |
| Magazines | |
| Direct Mail | |
| Giveaways | |
| Web Ads | |
| Other: | |
| Other: | |
| Other: | |
| **Sub-Total - Advertising Costs** | |
| **Customer Service Costs** | |
| Bad Debts | |
| Collection Costs | |
| Customer Satisfaction Costs | |
| Bank Charges and Fees | |
| Credit Card Expenses | |
| Depreciation | |
| Public Relations | |
| Donations | |
| Dues and subscriptions | |
| Other dues | |
| Other | |
| **Sub-Total- Customer Service Costs** | |
| **Total-Advertising and Customer Service** | |

| Category #3<br>Insurance, Office Supplies, Professional<br>Fees, and Miscellaneous | Cost |
|---|---|
| **Insurance - Business** | |
| *or Use Subcategories Below* | |
| General Liability Insurance | |
| Workers Comp Insurance, Nonfield | |
| Vehicle Insurance | |
| **Sub-Total Insurance** | |
| **Office Supplies and Postage** | |
| *or Use Subcategories Below* | |
| Office Forms | |
| Copy Expense | |
| Computer Expense | |
| Postage Expense | |
| **Sub-Total Office** | |
| **Professional Fees** | |
| *or Use Subcategories Below* | |
| Accounting | |
| Legal | |
| Consulting | |
| **Sub-Total Professional Fees** | |
| **Miscellaneous** | |
| Licenses and Bonds | |
| Meals and Entertainment | |
| Rent - Building | |
| Real Estate Taxes | |
| Uniform Rental/Purchase | |
| Other Office Equipment Rental | |
| Repairs and Maintenance | |
| Small Tools | |
| Shop Supplies | |
| **Sub-Total Miscellaneous** | |
| Total | |

| Category #4- Training, Utilities, and Vehicle | Cost |
|---|---|
| **Training and Education** | |
| *Or Use Subcategories Below* | |
| Travel | |
| Office Employees | |
| Field Employees | |
| Senior Management Training | |
| Team Building Training | |
| **Sub-Total Training and Education** | |
| **Utilities** | |
| *or Use Subcategories Below* | |
| Office Telephone | |
| Cellular Phones | |
| SaaS- Software as a Service | |
| Water | |
| Gas/Electric | |
| Garbage | |
| Other Utilities | |
| **Sub-Total Utilities** | |
| **Vehicle Expense** | |
| *or Use Subcategories Below* | |
| Fuel | |
| Electric Vehicle Recharging | |
| Maintenance | |
| Lease Expense | |
| Purchase Expense | |
| **Sub-Total Vehicle Expense** | |
| Other: Software | |
| Other: Tablet Computers | |
| Other: | |
| Other: | |
| **Sub-Total Other Expenses** | |
| **Total: Training/Utilities/Vehicle/Other** | |

| Summary-Total Overhead-Categories 1-4 | Cost |
|---|---|
|  |  |
| # 1 - Salaries |  |
| # 2 – Advertising and Customer Service |  |
| # 3 – Insurance, Office Supplies, and Professional Fees |  |
| # 4 – Training, Utilities, Vehicles |  |
|  |  |
| **Total Overhead** |  |

So now that you have these categories and have plugged in your numbers, what conclusions have you drawn? One of the revelations could be that you didn't realize what it took to cover your costs each and every year and you could take this information to a more detailed analysis of each month, week, and day.

You can also draw the staunch conclusion that while you believe you're selling solar, you can see that you're selling overhead first. Second, you're selling labor. Covering these baseline items to reach a break-even point is something you should verse forever to memory. In the next chapter, we will allow you to look at your productivity and weave it back into the overhead as they are closely tied together in coming up with the selling prices for your goods and services.

# CHAPTER SIX

# PRODUCTIVITY

As you can see from the budgeting exercise, a lot goes into your company's support structure, and when you factor in labor productivity it offers perspective on the level of detail it takes to be in business. One thing that usually jumps out at people is that they might not be charging enough for their products and services. Second, they don't know how productive their field teams are. If they have to go back to job sites beyond the allocated time, how much money are you losing that you previously didn't allocate for that job?

Quite simply, it's all about productivity or, said in a different way, effectiveness. We all know that things happen in business that are beyond our control and that can impact our effectiveness. Installing something incorrectly, waiting for a customer, a part, or another employee can affect billable time. Sometimes a new employee needs basic guidance and direction to do their job. Other things like training time and unbillable travel time will seep in to the average day. This causes you to pay someone for 8 hours of work when they are only productive for 6 hours.

This happens to everyone, so don't feel bad. Keep an eye on the hours you allocate to a project compared to the estimated time and share the information *before* the project starts. Don't let 6 hours go down to 5 or less and then continue to lose money on each job. As a reaction to this, many businesses will resort to hiring more salespeople hoping to sell their way out of the problem, and this often creates more challenges. We will dig into this more in the chapter on shared accountability, but this is where the dialogue should start. Productivity needs to be considered at the budget level and tracked and adjusted along the way.

I know people in business understand this, but they just don't do the math or understand the impact and influence this has on the core of every business. The other perspective is that they don't want to know, and those businesses are usually your competitors who are racing to the bottom. Don't follow them.

In our modern society, business seems to move at a more brisk pace than ever and making time to think through this simple basic exercise can be trivial. However, not knowing or understanding this can severely influence a company's ability to forecast the amount of labor hours that is budgeted for a solar project, whether or not it is a residential project or a utility scale project.

Another perspective is to do more than just share the information. When benchmarks and hours are hit on the budget, the employees can be rewarded as it will reinforce what you are trying to see in your company. We will drill down to this in another chapter and will show you examples of how to manage and achieve this.

Since we're on the topic of labor, it's time for the second phase of the work in this book: the direct labor. We will focus on the labor statistic now, as we have done the budgeting for the company. While you might not track all of this today, try to make it a habit. As Aristotle once famously said, "We are what we repeatedly do. Excellence, then, is not an act, but a habit."

| Category | Item |
|---|---|
| **Step # 1- Wages and Taxes** | |
| Installer-1 Person (productive people at your company) | |
| Installer's Hourly Wage | |
| Union Dues-if any | |
| Taxes- FICA- 6.20 % | |
| Taxes-Medicare- 1.45% | |
| Workers Comp Insurance-8.0% (this varies) | |
| State Unemployment Insurance-2.0% (this varies) | |
| Federal Unemployment Insurance- .12% (this varies) | |
| Subtotal-Nontaxable Pay | |
| Total Direct Labor Cost | |
| **Total Direct Labor Cost per Day** (hourly x 8 hours) | |

| Step # 2- Time Off | |
|---|---|
| **Step # 2- Time Off** | |
| PAID Vacation Days- how many do you pay or get? | |
| PAID Holidays- how many do you pay or get? | |
| PAID Sick Days- how many do you pay or get? | |
| Other PAID Days Off- how many do you pay or get? | |
| **Sub-Total Paid Off** | |
| Vacation Days-NOT PAID | |
| Holidays-NOT PAID | |
| Sick Time Days-NOT PAID | |
| Other Days Off-NOT PAID | |
| SUBTOTAL NOT PAID OFF | |
| **Total Days Off per Year** | |

| Step # 3-Cost per Available Work Day | Item |
|---|---|
| Annual Work Days-52 WEEKS x 5 DAYS | |
| Total Days Off Per Year-from time off- In step # 2 | |
| AVAILABLE WORK Days-Days off- subtract annual days-total days off | |
| Total Paid Days Off-from Step # 2 | |
| Hourly Base Pay | |
| Annual cost to the company for paid time off-Hourly base x total paid days off x 8 | |
| Cost per hour- divided by available work days | |
| Cost per day- divided by available work days | |

| Step # 4- Total Sold Units per Day/per Installer | |
|---|---|
| Available Work Hours- In a year | |
| Unbilled Travel Time | |
| Standby Time | |
| Time Charged Over Quote | |
| Warranty - Tech Error | |
| Warranty - Material Failure | |
| Training Time | |
| Other Time Off | |
| **Total Unbilled Units** | |
| **Total Sold Hours Per Person Per Year** | |

| Step # 5- Billable Efficiency or Effectiveness | Item |
|---|---|
| Person's Billable Efficiency | |
| Percent of the Available Time That is Unbilled | |
| Unbilled Person's Time as a Percent of Billed Time (this needs to be recouped!) | |
| Total Direct Labor Cost Per Hour | |
| Time Off Cost per Hour | |
| **Total Cost** | |
| Unbilled Person's Time as a Cost Per Hour | |
| **Total Sold Hours per Installer per Year** | |

| Step # 6- Calculation of the Breakeven for Person | |
|---|---|
| Total Direct Cost per Person | |
| Vacation and holiday/time off | |
| Unbillable time cost per hour | |
| **Total Direct Labor Cost per Person** | |

We now know our overhead costs, direct labor costs, and unbillable costs. We can take all of our costs we need to recover and divide this by the total hours we can bill out for our productive people. In this case, it's usually a journeyman, the people or person in the field that are doing things like installations.

Simple math: the total costs to recover divided by the total hours we can bill our customers. This is the first step to just break even, but we want to make a profit too! So, Overhead Costs + Direct Labor Costs + Unbillable Labor Costs = what the company needs to recoup to just "keep the lights on," i.e., to remain solvent. Take your total productive field labor and divide this into the number to determine what your break-even is. You should now be able to see why keeping score is critical. You can and most likely will be able to make money on materials, but can you always count on it?

# CHAPTER SEVEN

# BREAK-EVEN

This chapter contains a break-even calculation table that you can use. You will need to grab the information from the previous chapters, so flip back some pages to get the data.

| | |
|---|---|
| Enter in the Total Overhead Costs | $ |
| Enter in the Total Direct Labor Costs | $ |
| Enter in the Total Unbilled Labor Costs | $ |
| Total Cost to Recoup | |

| | |
|---|---|
| Enter in the Total Costs to Recoup | $ |
| Enter in the Total Hours We Can Bill | |
| Divide the Total Costs to Recoup/Total Hours We Can Bill | |
| Break-Even Cost per Billed Hour | |

| | |
|---|---|
| Enter the Available Work Hours per Year | 2080 |
| Enter the Amount of Hours You Can Sell—from Step #5 | |
| Enter the Billable Efficiency or Effectiveness—Divide Step # 5 by 2080 | % |

How do these numbers compare to where you are at now? Did you find any surprises?

Post these numbers on a dry erase board or have them in your business plan binder and check them periodically to do the "sanity check." Flat screen TVs are relatively inexpensive today and these numbers could be posted as a screen saver to scroll some of your metrics for the company for all to understand and to encourage feedback.

# BREAK-EVEN FIRST

Do you actually know what your break-even is at your company? Since we all get better at doing something with repetition, let's talk about some basic things that will eventually get us to our gross margin at our companies.

When an hour of labor is factored as an example, you are calculating the cost per hour, taxes, vacation, holiday pay, and unbillable time represented as a dollar amount. This needs to be added to the direct labor costs per billable hour to come up with a baseline cost for an hour of labor. You will then need to take your total overhead costs of your company and spread them across all of the available billable hours of your employees.

When we spoke about this in the previous chapters about an installation person being approximately 75% efficient, at $30 per hour, it will probably cost you closer to $50 per hour including all the items we discussed in the previous paragraph (unbillable time, vacation, holiday, training, etc.). When you take into account the total overhead costs divided by number of people in the field, this costs per billable hour will vary anywhere between $50 per hour up to $100 per hour based upon your overhead costs, which will vary from company to company. So in this example you can see how your break-even for labor is a minimum of $100 per billable hour, before we even plug in your desired net profit margin.

I believe that we must fully understand this concept, and many companies are not doing as well as they believe they are because they don't know what they're break-even costs are. They don't measure or manage their field workforce and often pray that they're going to make some kind of margin on their materials.

The importance of striving to reach 25% minimum gross margins doing installation work is a critical metric to watch and maintain. Historically this is the number, after all the bills are paid, that needs to be the selling price for your goods and services to survive. Not knowing your direct costs will cause you to unknowingly go out and try and sell more work at *any* margin just to fill the hole in your income statement. Remember—revenue does not equal profit.

But before I stick to my 25% minimum gross margin edict, I want to express to you that if you reduce your overhead and partner with other firms, the math could be a little bit different. You quite conceivably could reduce your minimum gross margin because you'll have less overhead to manage and cover and invariably have lower break-even costs per day. This will obviously translate into less net income, but in a saturated marketplace, perhaps you need to do this from time to time to keep working.

This is something you should learn and understand, like tying your shoes, and it should be a natural thing you do in your business. This doesn't mean your employees and customers aren't important, as they are the most important thing. However, you need to be solvent to serve them so they can count on you for their paycheck and your customers can call you in the future when they need service. They don't want to call a phone number that has been disconnected.

Effectively managing your field people will change the dynamic of your profit margins. If jobs are being done with the allocated amount of time that's been assigned to them instead of going back to the job site multiple times, then gross margin can become less significant. You can have a higher gross margin percentage, but lose money on the job due to your increase in direct labor costs going up by not completing projects on time. This causes overhead to be burdened more on the project than you originally allocated.

# WHY IS ALL OF THIS IMPORTANT?

Well for starters, we need to know how long tasks take to do because this impacts how you and your staff allocate resources. Before I go into why it's important internally in your company, how about we talk about the externally facing reasons why it's incredibly valuable.

Consider the bank. If you have detailed planning and strategies that are outlined, like a tactical daily/weekly/monthly business plan, don't you think when you need a line of credit (and it's just a matter of when, not if), that they're going to give you the line of credit because you have a plan? Or consider the company that is considering acquiring your company? You may be able to negotiate for more money because the actual value is proven as you have a system that is constantly checking itself. Do you have a financial partner? If you've done any joint ventures, they also want to know how you're going to execute before they put money in the deal and partner with you. You can think about a lot of scenarios where this is applicable, but it does add value, so please carve out the time to do it. This is also relevant when your organization grows, so your next layer of management can accurately do detailed project planning, procurement, and sales management. They will be there to serve existing and new customers while simultaneously being ready to handle the next wave of growth while carrying a road map.

Today, in a very competitive solar industry, you need to know how to effectively manage your field team. This is so you can focus on serving your customers. You'll make more money if you keep your field team motivated and they are enthusiastic to work with you and in your organization; they will deliver the results you expect. What if there was a way to communicate with the field team (your installation department) that you have a certain amount of hours or days allocated to specific tasks and if they reach these goals, you reward on them performance? Give your people something they probably have never been exposed to or never knew existed. How about a "paying for performance" model of compensation?

This will influence your break-even in many ways, as by achieving more productivity in the calendar month, you now spread your overhead costs across more projects, allowing you to "share the wealth." We will go into this in depth in the shared accountability chapter, but this does influence your budget, break-even, and the culture of your company.

# BUDGETING, BREAK-EVEN, AND LOSING MONEY ARE CONNECTED

Let us say that your organization is growing like wildfire. You're hiring salespeople it seems each week. You're also looking for more people in the installation team to manage the additional sales that you're racking up. You get into a self-fulfilling prophecy of hiring more people, and you need to keep more people working as the impact of them staying home has just dawned upon you. Now you've taken on the *responsibility* for not just the employee, but also for their whole family. The multiplier effect seeps into your business now. All of these people are counting on you to lead the charge and to maintain a steady stream of work and be gainfully employed. Are you feeling the pressure?

## BREAK-EVEN AND THE PROFIT MYTH

Hopefully this will give you impetus to determine how large your organization is, how big it's going to be, and what you need to do to get there from here.

Just to keep this math equation simple, let's agree that you have a $30,000 solar system that you just sold, and your goal is to make 10% or $3,000 on the project. Your sales team is crushing it this month and in this particular job you didn't have anybody to go out to preinspect the project. You're busy and you're hoping this project did not need any additional work added to the proposal costs and that the project was relatively cut and dry.

As fate may have it you get that surprise phone call. You

just learned that you need to upgrade the electrical service coming to the house. The situation causes you to have a $3,000 expense that was unforeseen and not calculated because your team was too busy. You go to the customer and plead your case. They aren't buying it. They say you gave them a fixed, firm price and they don't believe they should pull any additional money out of their pocket for a host of reasons. You, being the good company, take it on the chin and do the project as proposed to save face and maintain your integrity.

We calculated that we were going to make $3,000 on this project, but now we are making no money on the project. So let me ask you, how much more work do you have to sell at the 10% profit goal in order to recoup the $3,000 you just lost? This might come as a surprise to you but many people that are in business often don't pay attention to this detail. Their focus is solely on sales numbers and not on the unintended consequences like the one described above, and they wonder why they don't make any money or why construction-related activities historically are in the 3% to 4% net profit zone.

Not only does this scenario happen frequently, but it's been shared with me many times, explained as "just one of those things." In the chapter on shared accountability, you'll learn that when sales and operations goals are in alignment this usually never happens. Sure there's ways to penalize a salesperson or anyone in the company chain of responsibility, but why even go into the penalty box to begin with, when you can have the culture of your company in alignment from the start. This gives you, as a business owner or manager, more time to focus on growing the business versus being a referee, making the money you deserve, and serving your community.

When your company goes through these essential math exercises and writes down their numbers, you have something to reference. If you use Excel to develop a comprehensive budget, you can fully see the big picture of where the costs go. You need to know all costs, from monthly rents or mortgage to what computers and phones cost to insurance and training. Until this happens, everything becomes an uneducated guess and the guess is often way far off what you expected it to be. If reviewing your budget needs to happen quarterly, then make the time to do it. If you are in hyper-growth mode, overhead could grow out of control unexpectedly, hitting the bottom line of the company negatively.

# CHAPTER EIGHT

# NEW RULES, OLD PHILOSOPHY

Do you remember the exercise for calculating the field teams' productivity? It's time to start talking to your field people and empowering them. Knowing their costs and what their productivity is for their effectiveness every day can be in *their* sphere of influence. Give them the information they need to be successful.

Be prepared for employee push-back. In my own business, there were certain individuals that resisted accountability like the plague. They didn't stay long. When a majority of people in a group can see the benefit of accountability to everyone—the customer, the staff, and the company—and the downside of not focusing on measuring performance, everyone suffers. As with mutiny on a ship, where the crew wants to get rid of the captain, there was a mutiny in my company for those that didn't want to share in the accountability.

Many jaded business owners believe that most people are just trying to get through the day. Perhaps at some companies, this is true. It could stem from the simple realization that this information has never been shared and therefore perception becomes their reality. You will be pleasantly surprised that when you share the information of gauging productivity a shift occurs in the company in many significant areas: from economically to culturally, things turn in the right direction.

Customers experience a higher level of attention, and you'll see a swing in positive feedback and referrals. This is not some *Harvard Business Review* case study, but an actual company: my own. There are many companies that can also replicate the models in this book and put them into practice and see the results.

I must return to the 75% idea that was discussed in the previous chapter, because this one concept that is worth thousands or maybe millions of dollars to you. Just like you should now understand that employees are effective 75% of the time, what if you created a budget that also reflected 75% of the time that the whole company would be effective? This is what I recommend to all companies that I consult with: develop a budget framework around company-wide productivity as it relates to a calendar month. If you become more efficient or effective over the course of a month, in the installation of solar systems, as an example, you get to cover more overhead and increase profitability at your company.

## HOW MANY DAYS IN THE MONTH CAN YOU DO THIS?

To keep the math super simple, let's agree that each month has a 5-day work week plus 1 day, or a 21-day work month to cover the months throughout the year. So if we take the 21 days and multiply them by 75%, we come up with 16 days in a month. If we build our budget, including all of our overhead expenses, and dovetail this with knowing that our field teams are also going to be 75% efficient, we can focus on covering our overhead in those 16 days. Yes, I know they can work overtime and we can add more days, but if you haven't calculated into a project the additional costs for overtime, additional insurance, and other overhead burdens associated to these additional work hours, you could again see a gap in your income statements retained earnings.

What I've learned in my own company over the last 10 years, as well as working with other companies that perform installation work is to look at an hour or a day differently as it relates to doing basic tasks. Instead of just focusing on what a cost per hour is to install something, you can focus on what a "sold day" is versus a "sold hour." Sometimes a day is longer than 8 hours. It could be 10 hours or it could be less than 8 hours, but it depends on the work and the tasks associated to those activities. If you knew that each field team, meaning one journeyman and one apprentice, was needed to install 16 sold days in a calendar month, could you easily explain it to them?

The concept of a *sold day* is simple and easy to understand, and the field people should understand this day in and day out. This removes the complications of understanding what is expected of them in a day and helps you manage their expectations, customers, your staff, and ultimately profitability of your company.

How do we define what a *sold day* is? In the solar industry, there is a new way of looking at how we define a day's activities. When I say this, I'm most specifically speaking to urban types of solar installations that are grid interactive. This does not mean that we cannot apply this to other activities, we simply need to define approximately how long any particular task or activity should take. You also need to get input from your field team on how long tasks take on average. Management and labor will hold each other accountable to the outcome.

If jobs are starting to take longer in certain circumstances, adjust accordingly.

A sold day could be as simple as this: If we believe that 1 kilowatt (kW) of solar can be installed in one day by one journeyman and one apprentice, then we can say that it takes approximately 12 to 16 man-hours per kW to install the system. This concept is essentially the foundation of a metric man-hours per kW installed.

Using this metric, you should be able to determine, within reason, how long it takes to do a 5kW residential system on a two-story home, just like a 500kW commercial system on a big box retailer. We will go deeper into metrics, but this does coincide with labor hours and also will merge appropriately into the shared accountability chapter. We all seem to learn via repetition and this section is worth repeating.

Most work activities that surround tasking, in virtually all work where labor and materials are concerned, can be applied to this modeling. Ask anyone who works in the service department at an auto dealership. It's been called "book time" at these companies: They know how long a transmission is approximately going to take to install, as well as every other tasks associated to working on a car.

We can do this at your company for solar. If we can communicate to our lead people in the field the simple premise that man-hours per kW will be used to determine a days' worth of activities, we can now more effectively, schedule, plan, and manage our businesses both internally and externally as our customers see us. This schedule can be put on a simple calendar that everyone in the company can understand and plan around.

Of course there are instances when a site situation can add more time to a project or perhaps take a little less time. Preplanning a site inspection and preparing for of all the conditions relating to the installation as well as having a well-trained, and well-prepared installation team is key. There is no substitute for planning and good communication. It is something that needs to be woven into the culture of your company and practiced consistently to achieve the desired results that you seek, every day, month, and year.

If you're following along, you notice after you hit that 16th sold day, the other 5 days after that are essentially covered in your overhead calculations. What I mean by this is if we built in our overhead over the course of 16 days, we technically have those other 5 days that can be calculated as pure profit days, and that money can be shared with the people that help you to make it all possible. But before you do this, you need to remember it's your job to make sure the pipeline is full with work every month. This idea can backfire if you have no work for 3 months and the overhead is static, like it usually is, paying out those pure profit days can be economically painful.

You also need to decide how much of those 5 days you want to pay out in compensation. Perhaps you decide to create a slush fund and after a specific amount has been accumulated, then you share it. In the chapter on shared accountability, I dig into a few straight-forward models on how to do this. Sometimes this approach is hard to digest most specifically as it relates to the solar industry because labor represents a smaller percentage of the overall pie chart of an installation. Therefore many solar companies end up trying to make money on material and often cannibalize the profit that they made on material to cover mistakes made in the allocation of labor on any (or many) project that they didn't want to track or keep score on.

I call this "making money in spite of themselves." What I mean is, *thank goodness* the price of solar panels dropped enough so that a company can actually make some profit on a job. As more and more markets get compressed due to companies piling in to do solar work, the ability for companies to count on making money from selling materials will diminish over time. They will need to focus on selling their overhead and assigning time to tasks for the field people to follow or they jeopardize their viability as a company.

By implementing strategies like man-hours per kW, consistently working on a budget, and measuring estimated to actual job costs you will sleep better and reduce your anxiety about the future. If you establish a system of verifying these numbers by the 10th of the following month, you'll have a better understanding of the health of your organization.

To get some free information on how to do these strategies more comprehensively, visit the back of the book; we have a special guide for you with website access to assist you with your budgeting needs.

# CHAPTER NINE

# CASH FLOW IS KING

It doesn't matter if you speak to Warren Buffett or a small mom-and-pop solar business, cash is king and cash flow is its twin brother. If we look at the anatomy of a solar project, as it relates to the ratio proportion of materials to labor in a residential or retail business solar company model, labor represents 10% or so of the project costs. Solar panels, inverters and balance of system items represent the lion's share of the remaining balance.

With the high capital, upfront costs of purchasing solar equipment, managing your working capital is vital to your survival and your ability to build your next project. Knowing how to structure payment terms with your customers, vendors, and potential subcontractors could mean the difference between being in business or not or having to turn down the next development opportunity.

Whether you're installing one system a week or five systems a day, access to cash to fund your operations makes all the difference. On larger scale commercial or solar farm projects, this is even more critical. The lack of adequate money in reserves has caused many companies, which I know and like, to have to take out second mortgages on their homes just to pay their vendors and their staff. Other notable companies in the country and across the globe have had to merge their operations into other larger companies that were more effective at managing their cash flow. Their growth and their inability to operationally execute day in and day out caused them to be put in this position. For some it was a blessing to merge with a strong financial partner and in many ways this is a positive strategic move. It makes you well-positioned in your market and allows you to pursue more opportunities that many could only dream about.

How do small companies deal with cash flow if they are trying to grow? Well, first off, this does not have to happen to you and your company. Each chapter in this book builds upon the other, so in the end you will know, at a base level, what it takes to keep the lights on in your business each and every day. Knowing your numbers will give you clarity and the ability to look at your business strategically. By developing this framework and culture within your organization you will be able to scale your business, and you will have a roadmap that you can replicate and grow from. Sure you might need to add more staff at the middle management level, but the foundation of what I'm discussing in this book is applicable as you grow.

To digress back to the chapter on budgets as it relates to this chapter on cash flow, think about when you need to go to the bank to apply for a line of credit to float the inevitable dips in the lifecycle of your business. Can you see the value of going through the budget worksheets and knowing your numbers? Believe me, your banker will appreciate, respect, and usually be able to provide you with a line of credit to fund your day-to-day operations.

Of course you also need to focus on all the technological changes that seem to happen weekly and that you're supposed to be an expert on. However, the business principles are what will bring you solar success and allow you to make a difference in your community. These principles will also be the foundation for your entry into other types of businesses, should you decide.

How should payment terms be handled for customers and vendors from a cash flow perspective? Structuring or restructuring your payment terms with your vendors is pivotal in understanding and effectively managing cash flow. If, in the past, you have had a tendency to front the money for your company's solar projects, then perhaps those days are over, which should also put an end to the economic grief for you and your business.

Paralleling the scope of work, as it relates to an atypical solar project, requires developing a schedule of values that is clear and concise that customers can understand. As you are growing your business, you do not always need be the "nice guy" or the bank for the customer. Sure there could be resistance from a customer, but you can outline for them, the "why" and chunk down a project's costs so they can understand how this influences your financial position and that impacts your ability to serve them.

Ask for the appropriate amount of money up front so you don't get stuck asking for it in the future at a time when you are feeling pressure. It's better to track a schedule of values that are predetermined in advance. This will set the expectation with you and your customer from the get-go, eliminate any surprises as to when payments are due, and will keep your accounting department sane. The bank will also be enthusiastic to see this in your contract documents as well as your accounts payable history when you need their support during your growth mode for extending the line of credit.

I want to drift back a second to a previous thought that will illustrate this point more succinctly. If sales and operations are working closely together and are incentivized on project completion, this will influence usually to a positive, your ability to even better manage your cash flow. This is because many companies that I do consulting for seem to be eager to go out and start a lot of projects but sometimes don't fully complete things 100%.

Whether it's paperwork for one missing item or late deliverables on a project, many minor problems can cause undue delays in receiving final payment for the project. Many business owners are eager to start a new project, and field teams as well as salespeople will follow the lead of business owners as they sign their paychecks. So discipline is the theme here and the ability to take projects to completion and not having to go back will also set in motion an accountability culture in your organization that will pay dividends for everyone.

But why does this happen in the first place?

If the sales and operations people could finish the job completely, meaning the last project that they were working on, they could have an incentive when the project closes out and is job-costed, then they would know what's in it for them. *What is in it for them* is also expressed as *what is in it for me.* People do care about others, but they really care about themselves. This is why setting up a system that cares about the "self" combined with the "group" is the most effective method for fostering the right activities and culture in your company.

When management just directs sales and operations to make more sales or just go start another "urgent" project, there is often a disconnect and a lack of congruency between these two groups. What is in it for them could be a form of a bonus payment for collectively achieving the goals on time and on budget. If they hit the man-hours per kW goal coupled with a zero incident of accidents, as an example, you reward accordingly. You define what it is and you'll see a shift happen in your company.

Tweaking your company's compensation strategy as well as behavioral traits and charting a new direction does require courage and commitment. If what you're doing now isn't working for you, you might want to look at one or all the strategies and tactics outlined in this book. They will measurably improve your cash flow and the culture within your company.

# CHAPTER TEN

# MAKING MORE MONEY

Of all the things we want from our businesses, making more money with less risk is perhaps the most common priority. Often this can be very confusing for many businesses, small and large, as the ability to make more money seems to be directly proportionate to the amount of sales that are made. It's true that until something is sold, nothing really happens, but there is more to making money than just more sales.

Focusing solely on sales is a recipe for disaster. Many people in business throw around numbers to each other very casually, perhaps it's an alpha male characteristic or just a flaw that surfaces every day. "How many million did you do last year in business?" Have you ever heard anybody speak like this before? I know I have, especially with other business owners, because we get lulled into this as a measure of success. While selling millions or having hundreds of employees can be a signpost for success, it can also be deceiving.

We will explore this idea more in the chapter on sales because this measure can be misleading. The heartbeat of any company is to make more sales. But it is what happens after the sale that gets solar companies and other companies into challenging predicaments. We wish it was that easy, as if sales were the only recipe, then everyone would be positioning to hire every salesperson known to mankind.

# ALL THE WRONG MEASUREMENTS

If you're making lots of sales, it does not always mean you're making lots of profit. You might need to fill your pipeline with more and more sales just to pay your vendors, your employees, or your taxes. It's like a dog chasing its tail.

Can you see why in some ways, that more sales are not always the best route to profit? You should be focused on *profitable* sales. Revenue numbers can only tell part of the story, as it relates to the health of your business. What you really want is a higher price-to-earnings ratio. There are many ways to make more money in your company. But would you rather work Monday through Sunday just to sell a relatively smaller, incremental percentage of sales of your products? How about spending more time with the people you love, doing the things that you enjoy, and recharging your mind, body, spirit, and making fewer sales but having more profits?

Not to go esoteric on you, but we all need time for renewal in order to be sustainable (remember, we are in the sustainability business). So when I reference making more money, the currency of health and family are priceless, and I encourage everyone to value those relationships in many ways, like all the riches in the world. This is why most large corporations understand that the salary of their top performers needs to be balanced with a compensation package that includes a generous amount of time off.

# RECURRING REVENUE

One of the strategies that I know you should apply in your business immediately is a form of recurring revenue. Anyone that has a home alarm system with a monthly monitoring service can understand what recurring revenue is for the alarm company. You pay them a monthly fee to monitor the system in your home as well as being there for you 24 hours a day, 7 days a week, 365 days a year. These types of recurring revenue businesses are so popular that we are now seeing local cable and telephone companies offering them as an add-on service and also bundling them with their existing services.

How can recurring revenue be applied to your solar business? It's hard to find many solar companies that offer any type of service plan to service the solar equipment for the customer. They often ignore the other electrical related items in the home for things that aren't even electrically related to the solar system but require annual or semiannually inspections or servicing. Both commercial and residential customers can use your services.

# MAINTENANCE AGREEMENTS

What kinds of services or maintenance can you think of? A few suggestions are a whole house electrical inspection including the circuit breaker box, smoke detectors, and GFCI receptacles in their kitchens, bathrooms, and outdoors. On a commercial or industrial site you could perform energy audits, lighting retrofits, replacement of air conditioning systems, lighting control systems using motion detection technology, and geo–thermal systems. The list is constantly changing as new technologies are right around the corner. Your customers are most likely not current with the updates in your field, so you can educate them while offering maintenance for their systems.

The list of electrical items that you could check and add value to your customer is long. If you are coming from another industry, what do you do now that would add value to your customer that they aren't receiving? Just knowing that they can contact you and count on you when they need it the most instills peace of mind. They want to safeguard their most expensive investment: their home or business and the people they care about.

If you are coming at the solar industry from another building trade, like HVAC or plumbing, and can offer multiple services under one company that provides maintenance agreements already, then you are probably familiar with the idea of servicing. You are adding value in the customer's eyes as many customers are willing to sign service contracts to maintain their equipment in their homes or businesses. Customers prefer to have that concierge experience: make one phone call and have one company service their needs.

The potential of steady maintenance work combined with sharing with your customers any new technologies or energy saving strategies with them will allow you to reduce the lifetime cost of the acquisition of this customer. We'll talk more about customer acquisition costs again later in another chapter as it hinges on another topic we will talk about that is not mutually exclusive.

We live in a service economy and people want to be served. People are very busy and want to know that what they've bought is going to be working for a long time. I believe this is a reason solar leasing has also taken off. Someone else is going to maintain the system or power plant for the life of the contractual relationship. Again, another opportunity for you!

One other way to make more money is to have fewer costs. Look into partnering with other companies that do similar work. While it might seem unusual to take this approach and work with potential competitors, let me explain further in a moment, after I describe the global climate for diversification of your business.

As you look at the marketplace today, and if you follow trends, you will notice that there are many areas around the globe as well as locally that are experiencing boom and bust cycles. This can have a significant impact on your business as governments change incentive structures that directly cause you as a business owner to potentially layoff employees overnight or in some extreme situations to leave an area altogether. Just read the newspaper, watch the news, or go to the Internet, the information is available for all to read. The conclusive evidence is that counting on incentives to support your business is precarious. Relying on incentives puts you at the whim of a legislative session where the business models you once had can be forced to change. Positioning yourself to have a backup plan can come in the form of a recurring revenue strategy to bolster your position in your marketplace. There will be a huge opportunity to service and manage the megawatts of solar farms already in service as well as the commercial and residential systems that might have been orphaned by their initial installation company.

# PARTNERING

Most people's initial reaction to partnering comes with resistance. There's a tendency to want to do it all, turn-key for your customer. It's a natural desire to manage everything under one umbrella. But what if there was another way that makes it a winning solution for all parties: your customers, your partners and you? The framework I'm about to describe will come from your experience, your background, and ultimately your strengths.

Take a look at yourself, as a business person. What are you best at? What do you enjoy doing the most? Are you happiest when connecting with customers and sharing information with them? Or are you happier running conduit, pulling wire, and installing solar panels and inverters? Would you rather be in the accounting department, or developing land deals for a solar farm? Do you prefer spending time crafting public policy at your local legislature? Clarifying what you're best at is never easy. When I say this, I'm often referring to the people at new or smaller companies. These are the managers that find themselves doing everything in a company. As your company grows, you can relinquish certain activities to others and this time of transition affects everyone differently.

In order to know how to structure a partnership, you need to know yourself first. If you are happier installing things but you want to learn new and better ways to do business development, you could eventually find people that want to install things so you can get out of that role completely. This is something that will require you to develop a systems approach to segueing from one role to the next so things are done to your satisfaction and standards. You also need to develop trust and instincts for finding people to replace you if you are to focusing on replacing your core competencies.

You need to get real clear with yourself and identify your strengths as they relate to your business. If you don't trust people even after you've given clear directions, and you get upset when things don't go the way that you expected, partnering will probably be challenging for you. This is seen often in many small businesses that are characterized as "one truck operations." They never want to grow because they think they can do everything the best and trust very few with performing the work. This is acceptable for some, but the likelihood of an exit strategy happening is slim. Or, you might just "own a job," as most entrepreneurs, managers, and leaders direct and inspire others while finding people to do the work that they used to do prior to their current role.

As we look at partnering further, what part of the supply chain do you want to really be in? If you're really good at connecting with people and you have a strong marketing background you might want to consider other electrical contracting firms that are licensed and insured and know how to install solar systems to be your partners. They could appreciate the steady stream of work because they might not like to sell work, do not know how to "bid" work, and are happy simply installing your work. The same goes for commercial solar companies. Find roofing, concrete, carpentry, and other relevant partners to work with to allow you to focus, keep your overhead low, and develop successful projects.

In an example of partnering, you will do all the marketing, advertising, design, and engineering and then outsource installations to a competent firm. You will have systems in place so they can go out and prequalify a project prior to you providing the customer with the final proposal so you can avoid unforeseen expensive add-on work that will surprise you, your partner, and your customer.

If you have been tracking how much time it takes to do installations, then you will know on average what it would take for an outside firm to do one also. In our industry today, there are many ways to compensate a partner for their services and often it can be done for a fixed, flat fee. If we use a residential grid-interactive solar system as an example, you can formulate a pricing structure with your new partner using a cost-per-solar-panel-installed method as an example. You and the installation partner will look at historical records over time in your relationship as well as in your own relationship with other partners or, if you do this in house, you'll be able to look at your own books to ascertain how long, on average, things take to install. You could also create ranges on system sizes: if the system is 1 kW to 5 kW, it is *X* dollars per panel to install the whole system. *Whole system* means everything: panels, racking, wiring, inverters, etc. You can also subscribe this thought process to any add-on work at a project. This can also be applied to commercial projects, but for these projects you will need to further define the work in its scope to delineate the activities that each party is responsible for, so there are no discrepancies to what is and is not included in the pricing.

Whether it's upgrading an electrical service to accommodate a larger system or installing anything in a home, services can all be priced out prior so that you have a clear understanding of what your costs are going to be, and this will eliminate 99% of the surprises. Figuring out what things will cost up front will also assist you in fixing the variable costs that often come up in projects. You can also create a flat-rate pricing structure for most of these activities, again to firm up any variable costs. Every company would like to know what their fixed costs are on a project to more accurately predict gross and net profits for planning purposes. This will help you keep your overhead costs low because you will not have to think about keeping your partner busy all the time, unlike many small and large businesses that have to think about this every day.

Having people employed at your organization can put a lot of stress and expectations on you as you must keep them working all the time. By finding partners, whether they are used for your spillover work or they are your sole source for installation work, or any work for that matter, it becomes a win-win situation. Sure, many will argue that you don't have any control over partners. Well if you think about it, you really don't have any control over employees or anyone else for that matter. It's not about fear but about mutual success, and you need to look at it like that. Expectations, if communication is there from the beginning, can be managed.

This is how companies grow, not just organically, but it's also how companies, like my own, are acquired. Larger companies are always looking to partner with companies that they believe are savvy, conscientious, and honest and share the same values. While it can be difficult for an entrepreneur to step back from his or her ego to look at partnering or being acquired, it can also be a big step in personal growth. Being nimble in the solar business today and well into the future will be the hallmarks of your success.

As you start to carefully analyze your numbers, through the budgeting exercise and constant activity at your company as it relates to sales and operations, you'll get more familiar with your numbers as they relate to subcontracting. What I'm driving at here is when you realize what it costs you to have staff and support them, direct them, manage them, and carry them when work is slow, you could see an opportunity to truly partner and/or subcontract out aspects of your work that you know and believe could be better managed elsewhere.

Sometimes companies offer their services for less than what you can do them for at your company. So there are times when going down this road is applicable and makes good business sense. Some companies just have lower costs structures for various reasons and by partnering, both companies win.

Historically in the solar industry the fourth quarter of the year is when tax credits usually drive the buying behaviors of consumers and that is when the work is intense. Incidentally, the last month of the year tends to be the most chaotic and ironically the time when companies and people would like to wind down for year-end celebrations. So partnering for success in the third and fourth quarters of the year is critical. Plan ahead for the rush of business that almost invariably happens, like a perennial event, in the last quarter.

# SCALING UP SUCCESSFULLY

Scaling up is perhaps one of the most challenging topics in business, especially as it relates to construction activities similar to solar. Our business is not like a factory where machines do most of the work and they can operate for 24 hours a day. Combining labor and materials in an environment that is unpredictable can be challenging, as each and every home that solar is put on is a bit unique, unless you're in a planned subdivision. The commercial and industrial side of the solar business can be like a factory, but you also have weather, logistics, and the people factor to contend with.

At the core of getting scale, it simply boils down to your ability to grow your company efficiently, but more importantly, effectively. I've mentioned this as it relates to productivity, but now I discuss it in the correlation to growth. What I mean by *effectively* is that you must be able to grow your business and make more money as a result of taking on more risk.

Unlike manufacturing, where they just add an additional line or increase the run on the machines from 12 hours to 24 hours a day and add another shift or two, this is a different ballgame altogether. Scaling up comes back to the idea of partnering and scaling simultaneously, or the other possibility is to buy a competing business to merge talent and gain more entry points to potentially well-established markets.

In my own business as well as companies I consult with, either sales leads or lags as it relates to the manpower requirements from field installers to project managers and the warehouse staff. This becomes challenging to budget when there is usually a lag occurring with materials due to the capital intensive requirements associated to the cash flow available to manage multiple projects simultaneously.

There is no easy answer to this complex and constantly evolving flow in the solar business. Sixty years ago, the solution to this was in the form of labor unions that effectively became a resource base to address this problem. With the explosion of solar across the globe, many of these labor organizations were a bit unprepared for the amount of work that blossomed as a result of incentive programs. This is why partnering has worked so well across different business sectors, like roofing and carpentry, that work closely with electrical contractors to orchestrate the installation of solar projects.

The advantage for partnering can also be seen with the large-scale solar farms that have been developed around the globe. They all became partnerships with different tradespeople performing very specific tasks as the work can be very specialist-oriented with the various demands for unique skills. Partnering didn't stop on the structured finance of projects either. Many deals were also done through partnerships with lending institutions, hedge funds, venture capitalists, insurance companies, and the like.

Making more money in the solar business can come in many forms. Organic growth methods (increasing services to existing customers) or hiring 100 people for your sales force are just some of the ways this can be achieved, but first identifying what your strengths are will trump traditional methods, which can be counterintuitive to how money is made in solar. If you're uncomfortable with any of the methods mentioned about scaling up and partnerships, I would strongly encourage you to, again, begin with a budget and manage labor costs as they relate to kilowatts installed. Figure out how much you can install in a calendar week, month, or year and have your company sized appropriately for the amount of work that you believe you can successfully perform and don't let your ego get ahead of your capabilities.

# CHAPTER ELEVEN

# SALES AND OPERATIONS

While it may seem obvious that sales are the most important aspect of your business, some things I'm going to talk about in this chapter will surely surprise you. Look across any business and anyone will tell you that it is all about sales. This seems to also be trending in the solar industry. Many of the large companies doing millions of dollars in sales usually have a larger sales force compared to other solar companies in this space that chose to keep their organizations small. Whether they are doing door-to-door solar sales, TV and radio spots, direct mail, trade shows—you fill in the blank—their visibility is hard to ignore and the numbers cannot be dismissed.

Solar sales are different when compared to auto sales or pharmaceutical sales for one important reason: *profit*! The people in solar sales are usually making more money than their companies. This is the complete opposite of auto and pharmaceutical sales, where the companies are making more money than the sales representatives, which is why those businesses are much more established and fortified.

Solar sales can be a very lucrative career, plus you can give back and serve your community. This is one of the anthems of this book as making a difference and making a fortune can happen for you. This doesn't mean that you need to be an environmentalist to feel good about selling solar. The traditional ways that we generate and distribute electricity are somewhat outdated, and making power where you use it is sensible. People who are in the solar business now can surely share stories with you about someone they know who was in another industry and went into solar sales. Most will state that it has been the most rewarding thing they ever did and they are now making a difference and a fortune doing what they love: helping people solve a century-old problem of how we use, create, and generate electricity.

Solar and other distributed generation technologies that are being implemented now will only improve in the future of a decentralized energy grid. There will be more opportunities for salespeople and companies that offer these services just as computers revolutionized how we work and do business today. We will see technological breakthroughs in energy storage that will be affordable or financeable, just like an auto loan or a small mortgage. The world will need you to help consumers understand the technology and how it works.

## THE SALES OPPORTUNITY

To give you some perspective on the opportunity to make lots of sales, we first need to look at where you're at on the map now. As you can imagine, each country, state, or province have different incentive programs available. To go into each one here would be painful for you and for me as they are constantly changing and adapting the programs to the conditions of the marketplace. There are many resources on our website with directories outlining the incentive programs that are available.

I will give you a framework on the opportunity of using government incentives in relation to retail or residential solar sales. I'm going to reference some arbitrary numbers for the discussion about how you can capitalize on the opportunities ahead of you. Technological breakthroughs are happening often, so where the future lies for solar is unclear. New products and new materials for generating electricity via solar can skew any numbers printed in this book, so we have to look at my example as a snapshot in time.

If we can arbitrarily say that a residential solar system is $30,000, and you have an established electrical contracting business, how many people can you connect with in a month, meaning, how many people can you offer a solar system to? This is also factoring in a robust incentive program in your area in this example as well. We are also going to assume in this example that you're established or are partnering with a company that is established in your area.

So if an average solar system is $30,000, can you meet four people a week or sixteen people a month? Can you close 25% of your business a month: $30,000 times 4 equals $120,000 per month in sales or $1.4 million per year in gross sales. If you had five salespeople doing the same amount, you would have a business doing $7 million in gross sales for the year. At 3% profit, that would be $210,000 for the year. On the commercial side, just add zeros to the average solar system and the close ratio to come up with your own numbers. Yes, we want to raise the profit goal and my intent and vision for you in reading this book is to triple that 3% profit goal. You can make it a reality by applying the ideas, tactics, strategies, and systems outlined in this book.

I can say with certainty that these types of sales are happening in solar each and every day across the globe. The question you ask yourself should be, "do you want a piece of the action"? There'll always be plenty of work and opportunities for the people in business that want it, it just comes down to how much do *you* want?

## SOLAR SALES REVEALED

So how lucrative are solar sales? Across the country I've seen quite a few different compensation plans for salespeople. I work with companies from coast to coast, but I've found one consistent element in their compensation plans. Salespeople are often paid a commission as a percentage of the total sale price. So if a solar system costs $30,000, and they make 5% of the sale price, the salesperson's commission is $1,500. How many systems they sell in a month can vary, but in very hot markets I've seen salespeople sell one every other day if their company has a good marketing plan and an operations team that can consistently execute on what has been sold.

Sure there are some months that salespeople aren't selling one system every other day, but many salespeople I know are making a six-figure income and are able organize their life much differently than a 9-to-5 job. This has many positive implications and benefits beyond the money that can be made. For many displaced workers who lost their jobs over the last few years, solar has become a gold rush of an opportunity for them as their hopes for getting employed in corporate America have vanished. Even if they were working in a sales role in the construction industry, solar can become a lifeline for them while being relatively easy for them to understand and relate to.

When starting out in solar sales, you need to decide what type of solar sales you'd like to do. Are you more interested in doing business with homeowners or are you more comfortable working directly with businesses and land owners? Both of those types of customers are very different and have different criteria in their buying decisions. Both residential and commercial buying decisions come from economics. They are both dealing with escalating utility bills and want to reduce them or make those costs as fixed as possible.

The incentive for a residential or commercial decision to go solar will also be based upon a payback or rate of return. In many places around the globe, the cost of solar power is equal to or less than utility power, which encourages people to make the switch because it's a decision based on straightforward math. In some instances, it's a better return on investment than the stock market, where the return is unpredictable.

There are also a plethora of environmental attributes to switching to solar, what we call in the industry, *externalities*. These are the benefits to using renewable energy that are often challenging to measure or to assign a dollar value to, yet we know instinctively there is an inherent value in them. Examples of this would be by generating energy at the source of use, you eliminate the transportation costs of oil, natural gas, and coal being delivered to a power plant.

So the training and skills you need to sell solar in each of these specific markets are a little bit different from each other. Knowing why people buy or don't buy is critical to your success. If you come from a sales or marketing background and used to sell roofing, siding, or other business-to-consumer products, solar sales will be an easy transition. If you used to meet homeowners at their homes and showcase or explain about your products and services, retail solar just might also be for you.

Learning about the economic benefits of going solar, the paybacks, and how solar works from a technical standpoint are things you need to understand thoroughly. If on the other hand you want to do more commercial sales or offer solar to land owners to develop solar farms, this is more akin to real estate development. Having a clear understanding of financial analysis is essential in explaining the benefits of switching to solar to these types of clients.

As I dig deeper into commercial sales, I'll group all commercial sales with industrial and also with the land deals that become solar farms, which could be 500 kW systems up to multi-megawatt systems. You are probably asking yourself, "Well how much money can I make selling solar in this space?" I know that I probably sound like a broken record, but it all depends. Just like I described residential solar having a wide range of compensation strategies, whether it be a percentage of the sale or, in solar parlance, represented as a cost per watt, solar sales seems to be all over the map in regards to how salespeople are compensated.

In some large companies, you get benefits as an employee versus being an independent contractor. This is a much better structure than having salespeople go from "feast to famine," which makes the sales cycle and the salesperson often unpredictable. I would always suggest, after you determine that someone is ready to come work at your company and are committed and not just interested, that they become an employee. They'll receive a base salary and benefits and usually a lower commission so there is stability in their life and at your company as well.

Many will argue this, as their goal is to grow their businesses through sales, irrespective of any loyalty to their salespeople. I've worked with and have seen both models work effectively in many markets. Some consumers will go with the mom and pop companies and some want the national brands or 800 pound gorillas in the marketplace. Some people will prefer to do business with people they trust and know will be there after the initial sale is made.

Determine whether to focus on residential or commercial, then develop a plan because there are lots of ways to get there from here. All companies want to grow and make more sales than they did last month or last year, but you want to align yourself with a company that focuses on profitable sales and not just making any sales for the sake of making sales. A bad approach to sales hurts everyone in the company and has a ripple effect from your vendors, to your customers, to your brand, and to your wealth.

When choosing between residential and commercial sales, stick with what you are most comfortable with. If you are good in the consumer sector, do residential. If you are more adept at the commercial and large-scale projects, focus there. Both have benefits and drawbacks. Some companies do both exceedingly well, but often the divisions of their companies are radically different.

# HOW TO SELL SOLAR?

Before I talk about the methods, strategies, techniques, and processes surrounding how to sell solar, I want to offer a word of caution: Do it for the love, do it for the passion, but don't just do it for the money! People will pick up on your motives, and your authenticity will reveal itself to people, especially women, as they are masters of seeing through nonsense. Treat people as you would like to be treated and they'll respect you for that. They don't want an experience akin to buying a new or used vehicle at an auto dealership.

If you're not hungry enough, you will not get to where you need to be and not make the sales or be able to service your customer. When I refer to hunger, I'm referring to genuinely and sincerely wanting to help others. That is a hunger we should all want: to serve others.

Sales, or "assisted buying," is all about giving people information and letting them decide. Sales or marketing is a role of a teacher or educator. We are all familiar with the auto-dealership analogy and stereotype, but even their role in assisted buying and explaining the features of a vehicle has changed dramatically. This is due to the Internet providing granular information at anyone's fingertips and the information is only growing and allows consumers to be "self-educated." Many of your prospective customers will have done their homework and will know a lot more about solar than we might believe. Which is why I'm a strong believer in your personal brand being built as a source of information that people can trust and, in doing so, will result in referrals and continued business.

# THE HISTORY OF SALES

Aristotle lived about 2300 years ago but he was a modern-day salesperson back then. What do I mean by that? He recognized early on that sales, like a lot of things, is part art and part science.

He came up with these basic principles:

Ethos
Pathos
Logos

What is *Ethos*? Quite simply, it's your moral character, your credibility. Do you or your company have credibility? Let me give you a few examples.

"We've (I've) been in business *X* amount of years."
"We've installed *X* amount of systems."
"We've got a list of referrals/references."

As you're starting a relationship with a new customer and you're establishing credibility with them, you can ask them this very simple question after you've explained things like described above. "Would you want to work with a company like ours?" If they're looking for credibility or Ethos, this is a simple and straightforward question to ask them. If their response is a "yes," it will be the start of a dialogue to asking them a series of questions, whereas they can now begin to relate to you and consider doing business with you.

What is *Pathos*? As the name might suggest, pathos is the path or the persuasion that you will have with this prospective customer, or what I like to describe as a connection. Let me give you a few examples of emotional appeals.

Shared values and beliefs
Compassion
Storytelling

To go a little bit deeper, here are some statements you could be using with your prospective customer.

"I understand you have a high electric bill."
"I understand how you feel."
"Solar is proven; your neighbors have solar too!"

The above statements could lead to, "Would you like me to show you how you can start saving money right away on your electric bill?" Like with all questions that you ask your prospective customers, you are looking for them to say "yes." Everybody wants to know when they meet someone if they have established a rapport. If not then you have not made the connection yet. Asking "yes" questions or more appropriately, open-ended questions encourages engagement and causes people to make affirmative decisions about who they're deciding to do business with.

Aristotle knew this and you should too. As you can see, making the human connection has withstood the test of time and is probably woven into our genes.

*Logos,* as it sounds, is the logic involved in the decision-making process and usually the last step in seeing if there is a relationship that can grow further.

Let me give you some examples of Logos.

Facts
Statistics
Evidence

A series of questions that you could ask your prospective customer as you are going through your presentation with them about their lifestyle, their home, their utility bill, and so forth will lead you to this part of the relationship building. You will probably have discussed with them the products and services that you offer. Next, it would be a great opportunity for the customer to become the "engineer" and take ownership of the decision-making process by getting them engaged and involved in the decision-making process.

People like to buy and usually don't like to be sold to, so let them buy. In order for them to buy, they need to be making decisions.

One type of question to ask the prospective customer would be, "What system makes sense to you?" Since you probably have given them a few different options or choices, it's important for them to be involved in designing their own system. I'm not suggesting they are going to be doing the design work, as in using AutoCAD or some design software, but I'm referring to what I described earlier as building rapport and having them claim ownership of the system that they want. This is for a residential or commercial system.

I know this sounds overly simplistic as there is much more to this but if you follow this simple formula you will be getting the opportunity to be able to do three simple things: 1)relate,

2)connect, and 3)deliver. If you can relate to your customer (Ethos) and connect to you customer (Pathos) and deliver to the customer (Logos), then these are the steps that will allow you to earn the right to offer your products and services.

Don't dismiss this advice by thinking you cannot do it; we all do it each and every day whether we are aware of it or not. I think if we separate the idea of selling and focus more on relating, connecting, and delivering, it will reframe your brain to what you believe about sales or assisted buying. Remember, you are there to give them information and choices and let them tell you what they want.

# STORYTELLING

I mention storytelling because, at its core, it will always be the most memorable thing that anyone will remember about you. Yes, I recognize that the technical things are important but I can assure you that they will not be the most memorable. Recognize that the prospective customer is buying *you* and not a solar system. This applies to anything that is sold in the universe. People will always buy from people they like, trust, and relate to.

To break down the reasons why the customer is buying from you, 20% of the sale is technical knowledge or skills while 80% is "why" and "how." I know that this sounds unusual but it's true. Sure you will be selling solar systems to engineer types that want to know all the technical aspects, but just be mindful of the fact that if the customer is an engineer, and if he or she does not like you or trust you, no matter what you tell them technically, they probably won't be doing business with you. They'll find the person that they relate to and can connect with first.

If you as a salesperson don't have all the technical knowledge that this person is asking, you can always politely say those famous words, "*I don't know.*" You can then assure them that you will get back to them when someone from your company can provide the technical answers to their questions. You don't have to be right or a know it all.

# WHY PEOPLE BUY

There are many reasons why your customers want to switch to solar. The reasons could be anything from economic reasons, environmental reasons, geo-political reasons, and beyond. This is also one of those first few questions that you need to ask so you can determine where the direction of your relationship with this customer will lead. I briefly touched upon this earlier, but want to broaden the context here.

Here are a few reasons why people go solar.

Reduce operating costs-stabilize their electrical bill
Predictable electricity costs over time
Family or neighbor did it and they liked the results
Independence
Inheritance-giving home to family with no utility bill
Environmental-it's the right thing to do
Return on investment

The number one reason why people will buy from you is because you have a relationship with them. Yes, I touched on this topic before with Aristotle, but it deserves repeating. Remember this is a business-to-consumer product (residential solar), and it is built on relationships, reputation, and your company's brand. On the commercial side, it's going to also be relationship based, but it could also be about your track record and ability to perform, as there are hundreds of thousands to millions of dollars on the line.

I will tell anyone who is entering the solar business, or are already in the solar business, that the people they find to work in sales must have exceptional interpersonal relationship capabilities. They don't have to be hard closers because I know that those days of the hard sale are long gone.

# PREDICTING CUSTOMER OBJECTIONS

Objections can be multiple things, but at the core they are just more questions. Back to our friend Aristotle, gaining insight into your prospective customer requires you to ask a series of questions. I'm not trying to oversimplify how easy it is to sell solar but think about this for a moment when you're out in the marketplace looking to buy a product.

If you are shopping for something brand new and you're unfamiliar with it and you go to a store that has one, you ask questions. Maybe you're just shopping, or you could be gathering information and you might not be ready to make a decision if you're just doing your own research. But if a potential customer has invited you as a salesperson to their home, and you have done your job prequalifying them over the phone, the barriers to them making a decision are usually resolved before you've even gotten to the home.

So you can probably guess the number one objection: It usually boils down to one common theme—money! The upfront capital costs are a hurdle for anyone who is considering buying solar. These systems can cost tens of thousands of dollars and many consumers don't have that kind of money in their banks, and their lending institutions could be reluctant to loan them the money.

So what have you heard before as it relates to someone's objection to not going ahead with a decision to go solar?

"We can't afford it."
"It's outside of our budget."
"We are getting other bids, this seems expensive."

How does a salesperson deal with these objections? All people will want to hear are words of empathy. Understand what they're going through. Let me give you an example of a response that could be helpful. "Many people feel that way until they find out that that they're already paying for solar system but just haven't received it yet. May I have 2 to 3 minutes to explain?"

You see most people just don't have enough information or they have misinformation and need your help in facilitating and furthering their education.

This is the time to sit down with a prospect and learn more about what they know and dispel the myths. If people have not gone solar yet and the incentives are explained to them, they can see that over time the system will pay for itself with incentives and a reduced utility bill. Therefore they can now understand that they have "paid for system and haven't received it yet."

How do you counter when a customer states, "I'm thinking about it"? Refer back to Aristotle's thinking: You need to be able to develop the rapport before you even get to this objection. In the earlier part of the presentation, you should have asked the prospective customer, "do we sound like a company you'd want to do business with?" If you had gotten a "yes" early on, you can always go back to this question. If they did agree that you're the company they want to do business with and you answered all their questions then you can be confident to ask them a few additional things and not be overbearing or unreasonable.

Ask them *how long* do they need to think about it. Second, ask *what* are they thinking about. It might be something that you did not cover in your presentation that they are unclear about, which essentially distills down to that they have another question. Until you uncover this unanswered question, it will be hard to assess the situation.

From another perspective, you could be what I call the *first-in*. This means that this potential customer is getting multiple proposals, bids, or quotes from other companies. Sometimes this can be a challenging, especially if you have not been referred by someone to this potential customer.

Somebody who is "shopping" and undecided as to whom they'll be choosing as a service provider will always create uncertainty for you. When you look at the numbers as they relate to the costs of residential solar systems, a couple percent off a $30,000 solar system, for example, can be perceived as big savings in the eyes of the consumer. This is often hard to challenge, regardless of the products you provide, unless you can appeal to their objection. Ask questions when this arises to determine what they've been told by another company and what your company offers.

I will mention one final objection that comes up a lot, and no objection is simple to overcome. "We want to wait until we have more money because we hate paying interest on a loan." Neutralize this objection by framing it this way: "I know, but did you consider that paying a 4% interest rate would yield a 20% tax-free return? So if you don't pay the interest you lose 20%! Do you see why we all need solar ASAP? May I take a few minutes to explain this further?"

There are many ways and examples to show customers that investing a dollar in solar yields a far greater return than not investing. You can even reference the instability of the stock market or their mutual fund as an example of a risky investment versus going solar.

Think about this for a second. If your electrical bill is $100 per month, how much money do you have to earn to pay for it? It does depend upon your tax bracket but to keep the math simple for this illustration if you have a 30% combined federal and state tax bracket, you'll need to make $130 to net $100. This is a tool that you can use when explaining to your customers and is easily digestible by anybody without a financial background.

## OPERATIONS ARE THE IMPLEMENTERS

The anatomy of an operations team needs to be reinvented, in the way we currently associate to them and the significant influence they have on the successful outcome of any project.

We have technology today that can bring our teams closer. We can use smart phones, tablet computing, and ubiquitous access to the web all as a catalyst for a renaissance in how projects are built in the field and how information is shared across your company.

Let's break out who operations are and dig into all the steps leading up to a sale and how the sales team is supported prior to having a signed contract with the customer. At the very least, before we give a firm quote to a homeowner, we need to verify that the site conditions will accept all the things that the salesperson has proposed to the customer. This means that someone in the company needs to go out to the site to check a host of situations and conditions to verify things like the roof being in good condition and the electrical infrastructure being able to accommodate the proposed system size. Many elements can impact an installation. Yes, there are tools today like Google Earth and other products that allow a flyover of the roof, but most things require a site visit. In business, this person is a *site planner* or person that does a site survey, and usually this person would have an electrical or technical background. On commercial projects, this person could be an engineer.

After the site survey has been done and verified, the project planning and procurement can be put in motion. While it's not as glamorous as doing sales, this is often where the profit in a project for a company is gained or lost on a consistent basis. The operations team consists of project managers, supervisors, foreman, electricians, apprentices, warehouse staff, delivery people, laborers, and subcontractors. If we don't do a good job, as an operations team and organizing a series of tasks and activities, the likelihood of profitability is a gamble and almost like buying a losing lottery ticket. When you're counting on "hope," you should be counting on your team's ability to plan, focus, and understand project scheduling and providing a feedback loop to the company. Deviations from the original strategy on how the project is going to be installed can influence the sale of your goods and services in the future. Missing a critical item, like a service upgrade or a larger ticket item that you can't bill for on a commercial project, can wipe out any profitability that you envisioned or forecasted. Often, the bigger projects will have the more unknowns for new companies entering the market.

Refer back to the last chapter where we talked about profitability and making more money, and we also talked about partnering. If you don't know your budget at your company, you don't know what it costs each day to cover your overhead. If you don't have an effective scheduling protocol, your ability to forecast the amount of sales in ratio and proportion to the amount of field people you have is also a guess. Add in the field team's effectiveness in the installation of your products and services, and your company could struggle to be in sync as it relates to the sales and operations departments and ultimately the execution of your projects. I believe that in many companies, sales and operations become archenemies when they find themselves disappointed with each other's performance and expectations. This further causes dissension in your company and distracts everyone from the goal of serving your customers and making a profit.

This problem is consistent across the country and probably the globe and really doesn't need to be that way if sales and operations can work more closely together. When I refer to this, I am speaking on a retail level (residential solar sales). Compensation could be incentivized on the profitability of each job. A majority of the companies today have no correlation in sales and operations on an economic accountability level. What I mean by this specifically is that salespeople receive their commission, regardless of what happens in the operations of the company. Many will argue and say that it is not the salesperson's responsibility to have the operations people be efficient or effective.

While I agree that it is not their responsibility, if the sales team or individuals on the sales team are consistently selling "bad paper," where other salespeople on the sales team are consistently selling "good paper," yet there is zero incentive for the "bad" or the "good paper," then there will be a disconnect at your company. Good and bad paper simply refers to selling and closing your customer, but the project can't be built for the price that was quoted to the customer. Invariably, the company ends up losing money or making money on this factor alone. I see this from coast to coast, so I wouldn't be surprised if it wasn't happening at a company in your area, as we seem to proliferate and export ideas from company to company and they know no boundaries.

## GOALS IN OPERATIONS

On the flip-side, operations people should also be given goals, as discussed in the previous chapter. They can be held equally accountable as are the salespeople. Meaning if they have jobs that have $X$ amount of hours for $X$ amount of days allocated to them, and they reach or exceed those goals, they should share in the upside. This applies to the salespeople at your company. If they're selling good paper, shouldn't they also be rewarded? I think if you surveyed 100 companies, they all want to pay more, if only they had more to pay.

But what has happened in the industry is that companies have gotten lazy, plain and simple. They just assume pay a commission and pay by the hour and have jobs sold and jobs installed. If they make money, they do, if they don't make money, they yell and scream and become jaded and it becomes an endless cycle of disassociation, dissatisfaction, and often resentment. Owners become complacent and also just want to get through the day and wonder why they got into business in the first place.

Why I present this idea of shared accountability is because it's all about raising your standards. Taking 100% responsibility for things is not something our industry is comfortable with as we are often herded together and stay in the tribe with how we run our organizations. If it's broke, we know we need to fix it, maybe sometime in the future, when we have more time, resources, or the right people. It doesn't have to be this way, but it does take courage, retraining, commitment, and buy-in at all levels of the company in order for positive change to be adopted and implemented. By not doing it, you get the same old same old, and it's easy to stay the same as our lizard brains seem to be wired for fear versus creativity, congruency, and a fresh perspective.

Yes it does take effort to implement these ideas, but are you happy with the results you're getting now? If you're content with sales and operations not working together, low or no profitability, high stress, and looking like you're actually running an adult daycare center rather than a solar company, this is entirely up to you. Just imagine for a second what it would be like, if sales and operations truly enjoyed working with each other.

Wouldn't everyone benefit if a salesperson didn't try to close the deal without an important piece of information that should be run by someone more technical than them prior to giving the final proposal? Do you believe that if a system was in place where everyone knew they could make more of a percentage of the project in terms of compensation that their behavior would change? Let's also put our feet in the shoes of the operations people. What if they knew that they would also be compensated above and beyond their hourly pay if the project came in profitably? Instead of not wanting to talk to the salespeople they would be calling them on a more frequent basis and supporting them with any technical questions that they might have in order to prevent a job from losing money before it's even started.

It is these behaviors and habits that have to be looked at with an open mind because they can change the course of history for your company as well as your customers. In a lot of ways, I'd like to see this revolutionize how many industries around the globe work. Companies should pay for results and reward excellence.

As with all human nature, people like to talk and share what they see, hear, and experience working with you and your company. What would you like them to be talking about when they're thinking of bringing up your company's name and the people that work there? I'd like you to look at sales and operations from a new perspective. They can work together and be the most influential part of your company, with a new approach to team work and compensation. Aristotle figured it out 2300 years ago and a lot hasn't changed about how we interact, but what has changed is the ability to leverage technology to pull it all together. Shared accountability will boil down to one simple facet: are you willing and are you able?

# CHAPTER TWELVE

# SHARED ACCOUNTABILITY AT WORK

"It's not my job!" We've all heard this before. It doesn't matter if it was at the dinner table when we were 12 years old or while we're working at our current company, we have accepted this response as the norm. When you apply for a job, they give you a job description. This job description is supposed to help you understand what is expected of you at the company, in a clearly defined role and function, but our modern work life has blurred the lines of role and function in a company. Our country has drifted away from the manufacturing base that used to be where role and function was critical to the success of building something like an automobile. There was a time and place for this, but that time is gone and never to return to our shores. This is not to suggest that you should not have a job description or know what your role and function is at your company.

## EVERYONE'S JOB

The barriers of "it's not my job" must be broken down to "it's everyone's job" in order to see the successful outcome of a project and to serve our customers. Now this does not mean that you pull somebody from the accounting department and send them to put solar panels on the roof of a two-story house. What I am saying is that our society has gotten very used to the blame game, with statements like "that's not in my job description." This attitude has eroded teamwork in companies and ultimately may have cost many companies future business. It also has caused talented people to leave great companies as a result.

This is why a new paradigm has to exist in solar businesses today. It's not just to be effective but to be a legendary organization that people are proud to work with and to contribute in to serve others. I'm not mincing words here but pointing out a new direction for your company in a changing world. Commodities never become legendary. Don't be a commodity.

# OWN IT

Shared accountability can come in many forms but at its core, it will always come down to teamwork and owning problems when you see them happen and dealing with them individually or collectively as a group. In general this is not in our human nature, especially when it comes to people making mistakes and wanting to hide the mistakes, because they don't want their egos bruised. Being embarrassed, for anyone, is not a pleasant emotion to experience, and no one wants to be identified as the root of a company's problem. The truth is that we all make mistakes, but we must own it and let it go. It seems like we're hardwired to avoid admitting to mistakes, and we perform damage control that surfaces in many peculiar and often ugly ways.

Why don't we have shared accountability in the workplace today? I can give you one of the reasons why. I'll also give you a reason why sales and operations, or just shared accountability in general, isn't implemented, encouraged, or often discussed.

# HUMAN NATURE

It goes back to what I just said in the previous paragraph about human nature. We have no problem opening up a spreadsheet and trying to get a better quote from our vendors for materials, because this is relatively noninvasive and we don't have to work with them on a daily basis, but we do have to work with our staff and teams. What I'm driving at here is it's easier to deal with a vendor and work tirelessly on getting the best price for our widgets, but we do not dedicate time to working with our own people. It's unfortunate, but you can decide to change this today.

Many people feel very uncomfortable with setting expectations, holding people accountable, and encouraging them to reach their goals, or for that matter, having any goals at all. My challenge to you is to send someone out in the truck and tell them they have X amount of hours or days to complete a project. Can you do it? If not it's because you don't want a confrontation. You don't want to live in a state of constant conflict or feel like you're micromanaging everything that they do. Even if you're not, perception can be reality, without explanation. You need to have the courage, to be bold, and be a leader and set this expectation early in your company and be consistent. When this is implemented, there'll be less of *them versus us*, and more of a team environment.

Let us look at an example of rewarding accountability in your company. For the sake of simplicity and assuming we've already dated the costs of a project, we will assume a few factors.

3kW residential system
Assume the system cost at $5 per watt
Commission of 6%= $900
Install goal of 15 man-hours/kW to install, 45 hours

If the team hits the goal or beats the estimated hours, this time and money gets tracked and goes into a "banked" account of time or days. This will be measured over the course of a month, and we want to verify in the next month that we have no call backs or reasons why we need to go out to the site that have to do with workmanship or other things that are in the control of the field team.

Operations people usually receive "zilch" for a job well-done and usually only hear about the job when it didn't go well. But what if there was another way? I'm sure the salesperson would be interested in making more than 6% or whatever the usual commission is at your company. And I know the operations team would enjoy some additional compensation of let's say 2% or $300 in this example. Would this really cost the company an additional $600?

This depends on a host of variables, but as we "back up the truck" a bit in this dialogue, we really start talking about budgets and overhead for the company. From all the research I've done and personal experience, the overhead for the operations team could be $1,500 per day or more. Obviously your numbers might be different depending upon your cost structure. If the overhead is $1,500 per day and the project was completed in the time estimated, then the company made money, even after paying $600. If the job dragged into the next day, you can see how they would lose money in more ways than one. The overhead wouldn't be covered for the second day because we didn't allocate it to the job originally and our schedule has now slipped and we can't serve more customers that month than we expected to. While this is just one illustrative example, the intent is to drill down into what is job costing. You need to know ahead of time what your costs are each day for your field crew to install a project. If you keep score and track activities associated with tasks in your company as they relate to the field activities, you'll have a lot of these metrics already sorted out and ready to implement.

If you're not tracking these types of activities, start today. Absent of any goals or feedback from the company, we miraculously expect certain behaviors and habits from the people in the field but we often find ourselves keeping them in the dark about their effectiveness. Conversely we tell salespeople to just go out and sell. We don't talk about profitable sales and how important they are to the company. If you shared this information with the salespeople they would get a clue about how long things take to install and how the ripple effect also impacts the existing jobs that they've already sold as well as future jobs that they've sold. By not sharing this information, it influences the installation schedule that they've been telling their customers.

There is no part of a company that is not impacted when information and goals are not clearly communicated. Equally as damaging is the separation of sales and operations, when they should be incentivized on results. If this means paying less of a salary, but rewarding excellence, then I encourage this. One of the benefits to implementing this type of strategy is that the company would be less inclined to take certain projects because they might hurt everyone in the company. That doesn't mean that management sometimes decides to take projects that might break-even or make a little bit of money, but armed with the information at least they can decide. Without any information they just get circumstances.

If your sales team and operations team had more goals of getting jobs done on time, on budget, and you actually make the net profits you calculated, you would see the culture in your company radically change. You should also factor in how your stress levels and home life would change. Could you see how this would not just improve the financial condition of your company but potentially allow you to lower your pricing of your projects? If you're more efficient or effective, depending upon which word you like to use, and you get more work done in a calendar month, you are in effect reducing your cost of doing business.

# MATH DOESN'T LIE

The math speaks for itself but I recognize that this requires effort. Many companies want sales and many companies don't want to do the math exercises that I'm describing here. They don't want salespeople mingling with the operations people. Sometimes they believe that they won't understand each other and that they have different goals. While on the surface this could be true, at a deeper level it's entirely false. People want to do well, feel significant, and be recognized for their achievements. It's the human condition that you cannot ignore.

Having the courage to even consider or implement systems like this are counterintuitive for many businesses today for the simple fact that they have not been exposed to these types of ideas or strategies and tactics to make their companies more efficient and more effective. They also haven't calculated the impact that the customer experiences when doing business with you. The customer wants the job done in a timely fashion and a job that's done right the first time.

They want to know that there are people on your team looking out for their best interest. Yes you can hire a project manager to get in the middle of the equation, which is often the case. For large firms, and I'm talking about companies with over 100 people, keeping score on profitability on a project by project basis could be construed as difficult to manage. In some ways, with more management, it will be even easier to track and follow; it will always come down to teamwork and good management. We can look to the military and see small groups of individuals working as a platoon, and in solar you can also see collaboration with groups of installation teams and sales teams working together for the common goal.

As you look to the future and think about today, how do you differentiate yourself in the marketplace? By having a new vision of shared accountability at your company, you will attract people that share common values like you. Being in business is about serving your customers in the most effective way you can while simultaneously having your team engaged in the successful completion of projects. Making money is not everything but when you don't have systems in place that can allow you to measure results, the inmates run the asylum and you will eat bread and drink only water.

Incentivize the sales and operations teams to focus on keeping the gross profit where it needs to be, from initial proposal to the end of the project. The initial snap shot of what the gross profit was to where it ended up can be in the team's control and influence. Yes, this does require educating your team on the *why* and *how* but this will always boil down to willingness and not an ability on any vested interested parties' position in your company.

If the company has a level of transparency that is understandable, meaning sales understands the gross profit prior to selling the project, and operations understands the amount of time allocated to a project's tasks, then it is relatively easy to communicate and measure these activities and share them with your team at a frequency that is reasonable. With modern technology and companies and individuals using smart phones and tablet computers, this information can be easily shared from both directions: the company and the team. This can happen daily if desired to meet the goals of the company and effectively serve your customers.

# CHAPTER THIRTEEN

# MARKET MY COMPANY

Marketing, at times, can be as elusive as Bigfoot. It works a little bit like Thomas Edison in his laboratory, constantly trying new methods and materials, time and again to create the incandescent light bulb. After a lot of trial and error, and after about 1,000 different filaments, he made the light bulb.

The good news is that the success principles for marketing your solar company are already proven, but you first need to answer this very important question: Have you ever stopped and surveyed what your customers want? Ultimately if we don't ask them what they want, how can we know what anybody else wants? Ask, stop, listen, and repeat. Let people tell you as they have needs, wants, and desires, but we often tell them what they need versus letting them tell us what they want. Take some time in your company and sit down with your existing customers and ask them the hard questions. Some of their answers might be difficult to listen to, but they will give you vital clues for you to take back to your company and apply.

Survey your existing customers and ask them how you did on a scale of 1 to 10 for your service experience with them. "Is your solar system working like you expected it to?" "What could we have done better?" "What would you like to see from us, if we could do it all again?" Listen for their concerns and don't take it personally. Recognize it as feedback for the next customer. If your company is not scoring tens, find out why, address the issue, take notes for your company meetings, and be sure to use customer feedback as research into your marketing efforts going forward. Sure there will be some who will never be satisfied and never give you the 10, but you still should have the courage to ask and be open to what their concerns were. Everyone is not your customer. The key takeaway here is to ask good questions and to not react to the answers but appreciate the message.

If you're just starting out, and don't have a marketing plan, we're going to provide one for you in this chapter as well as give you other strategies that are proven in every marketplace. Think of marketing like a calendar for what a retailer does. Throughout the year they are "campaigning" you. Look at a major clothing retailer, each season they roll out their winter, spring, summer, and fall products. They are always planning ahead. Think campaign! Are you campaigning all year round?

## SKIP THE YELLOW PAGES AND RADIO

Despite some of my critics, I firmly believe that the *Yellow Pages* are dead, they just don't know it yet. Google is at our fingertips with mobile phones and tablet PCs and widespread connectivity to the Internet. Online is where people are finding information about your company, your products and services, and deciding whether or not they should hand over their hard-earned money to your company.

People are bailing out on the *Yellow Pages* for some simple reasons, like not wanting to commit to a static marketing campaign for close to 2 years. When you look at the full cycle starting when you first have to make a commitment to your *Yellow Page* representative, it's a lengthy process. From the time that it takes them to print the book and circulate it, and by the time the book comes out and then up until the next year it can be almost 18 to 20 months, and you cannot change anything. A lot can change in 6 months and a heck of a lot more can change in the lifecycle of your modern solar company. This is why I would shy away from advertising in the *Yellow Pages* and put those marketing dollars that you budgeted for the year towards other things that can be measurable as well as adaptable to market conditions.

Have you considered radio? The frequency and the cost of reaching your audience, unless you own the radio station, can be very cost prohibitive as the listener needs to hear the message 3 times a week for multiple weeks for it to be etched into their cerebrum. This can really push your customer acquisition costs into the stratosphere.

# OPEN HOUSE

As with the popularity of open houses for Realtors, this marketing approach has also been very successful for solar. It is effective because it meets multiple needs for curious potential homeowners who are vacillating as to whether or not they should go solar.

The experience can be similar to going to a furniture store or some other place where they can look, touch, feel, and see it working in real time. It can help eliminate uncertainty in the prospective customer's mind as to how the system works and how it would look on their home. They need to be able to visualize it for themselves and this is a great conduit and setting for that experience to take place. Remember, their peers, fellow homeowners, will confide in them whether or not it's working! They will also tell them all about you!

If someone invested a lot of money in a solar system and they are happy with their decision, and it's performing as you've outlined in your contract and presentation, they will likely be interested in hosting an open house for you. But you will want to make it worth their time. Sure they want to be proud of their decision, but what if there was a way to thank them, economically, for hosting the open house? It might be an inconvenience for them and you also could share with them, a little about what it cost for your company to acquire new customers.

Would you rather spend thousands of dollars every month on a yellow page ad, or would you be able to ask your satisfied customers if they would be interested in having an open house while being rewarded for every customer that signs up after visiting their home? This is something that you can speak to them about and negotiate compensation for, but think even deeper about the likelihood of trust being built with people showing up to the open house. They are all probably close neighbors or were friends of close neighbors that would not intentionally steer each other wrong and would be grateful to know that they are receiving information at the open house that will increase confidence in their buying decision regarding who to choose as a solar service provider.

# UNDERSTAND HER FIRST

Let us consider the nature of men and women as it relates to the open house experience. It meets both of their needs simultaneously, yet they are both looking for different things. This idea and the difference between men and women is not intended to be polarizing, as these are general ideas and feedback from clients as well as my own experience of surveying clients over the years. There are many households with single parents and other nontraditional families, but statistically this is what we usually see in the marketplace.

Men are looking for technology: the digital displays, the data, and how it works; we are fascinated with blinking lights and gadgets. We also enjoy the bragging rights, almost like having a classic car in the garage. For the women, they want to know how it will look on the house, what is the cost, how they are going to pay for it, will the roof leak, will my girlfriends like it, will it really save me money off my electric bill, what are the tax credits, and are you trustworthy. This is not to suggest that men don't think about these things because most of them do. Women usually control the finances in the house and pay the electric bill, which makes them the authority in the house for the decision to have solar or not.

# IS DIRECT MAIL STILL EFFECTIVE?

Marketing is perhaps the most difficult thing for me to recommend to anyone as I've always been a fan of referrals or even providing finder's fees to bridge a relationship. Using a shotgun blast of money towards things that will give you visibility in the marketplace, can be helpful but should be used as sparingly as possible as their effectiveness is difficult to measure.

If you're new and trying to get the word out about your organization, then a relatively inexpensive route would be to do a direct mail campaign. This can be anything from a postcard to a multipage newsletter with information that could be helpful beyond solar so it could contain added value and not just look like another piece of junk mail showing up at their door.

When you implement direct mail pieces, it is not a one-time thing, but a campaign. The campaign consists of more than one touch point for your customers over a period of time. You can also consider a direct mail campaign with an offer that has an expiration date. This will be a call to action to the prospective customer, in order for them and you to move from interested to committed.

Graphic artists today are very easy to locate online and are relatively inexpensive to hire to provide these services for you. There are a host of freelancing websites, local design shops, and specialty shops that focus specifically on direct mail marketing campaigns for you that can be done quickly, professionally, and economically. There are also service companies on the Internet that can also do this in a print-on-demand fashion, which is very reasonable.

# PUBLICITY: GOOD DEEDS

How about doing something outside of what you do for business? What kind of publicity could you get if, for example, you started to collect food from your customers or people walking in front of your office for a local food bank? You could use this opportunity to connect with your community and also get some good press from local newspapers and even TV stations, which are starving for good human interest stories.

You will also humble everyone in your company and help them become grateful for what they have, which is an intangible I recognize, but sometimes we need to stop, step back, and get some perspective. Pause for a cause. This will also be a great story that your salespeople can share with new and existing customers and it might actually encourage them to do to some significant things and increase their engagement with you and spread the word about the work you do and the causes you represent.

# PRESS RELEASES

Visibility in the marketplace, especially one that becomes saturated, means that you to stand out above the rest. An investment with a local PR firm can extend the reach of your brand and assist with press releases. Often this can be accomplished by yourself or even someone on your staff, as PR firms have relationships with government officials all the way down to the local newspaper. They can get you into meetings, get you on the news, and get you exposure, which is really what you want to do in the first place.

If you at first cannot afford a PR firm, then a less expensive solution would be to go on a subscription service that allows you to send out press releases relating to you and your company on a frequency that you deem appropriate. Whether this is one time per month, more or less, or when you have a newsworthy announcement, a press release can also provide you with reach to your audience for lots of reasons. From a positive perspective, many news organizations are looking for great stories beyond the train wrecks that they report on a daily basis. Human interest stories on the news or in the newspaper capture people's attention in ways that sears your company and your brand into their brains.

If you can afford the monthly retainer for a PR firm that is working every week to find ways to get you exposure and visibility, this will have a long-term positive effect on the perceived size and capabilities of your company. Again like most marketing, it's not easy to measure how well a campaign is going but at a certain size of your company, it seems like you need to explore every avenue for visibility. Brainstorm what is newsworthy that's going on at your company. Have you acquired, like in a sports parlance, a superstar that is now joining your company? Do you have a great human interest story? Did you raise money for the food bank, a homeless shelter, or give away free solar system?

Think about ways that you can extend your brand in the marketplace, and they don't have to be specifically related to the solar field. The methods can be parallel to the green space. You might want to go out and clean up the beach and make that newsworthy. Pick up garbage in a stream in your town. Teach children at a local school about renewable energy or another topic that is meaningful to them. Give a free talk on solar at a community center. The list is endless.

With community outreach you're only limited by your imagination and your ability to relate and connect with your community. It does require time and effort, but the benefits will always exceed the costs. There are other intangibles, which would be very hard to quantify, but is it okay to pay it forward?

# VENDOR PARTNERSHIPS

Is there a vendor that you do business with that you could partner with? If you are running a contest to give away a free solar system, another vendor that manufactures the products or distributes the products may be interested in donating some of the items that you need as part of a sponsorship. This could be an opportunity to increase their visibility and PR campaign. They don't have to contribute a lot of products, but just attaching their name to your brand gives them visibility in the marketplace as well. We see this in motion pictures today. Placement of products in movies happens all the time, and sponsorships are used in most professional sports.

Another way that vendor partnerships can work is through education. They often have training days that are sponsored by manufacturers and they're often looking for places to host events. So connecting with a local distributor, or partnering and sharing the cost of a hotel banquet hall or room, will also increase your visibility in the marketplace. You can invite people in the industry as well as other trade associations for free training or some other compensation structure.

# TESTIMONIALS

This is perhaps the simplest yet the most effective marketing strategy anyone can suggest. Word-of-mouth advertising goes beyond any print media today. Through social media today, people can comment on the Internet, on their websites, and send text messages directly to people giving feedback when they have questions about using someone's products or services.

This is why having testimonials, either written or in video on your website, is critical to winning over your customers. No one can underestimate the impact and raw power of someone recommending you to them. They're putting their reputation on the line and that is something that is near and dear to us all as we don't want to hurt our friend's feelings by recommending someone or something to them that will cause them grief.

Getting testimonials might seem difficult, but you need to just ask for them. If you've done your job and delivered on your promise there should be little or no resistance about receiving a testimonial. There should be little or no hesitancy for them to say, "How would you like a testimonial?" It seems that in the marketplace today that almost any product or service that we purchase, our expectations are in the stratosphere. When someone does delivery on their promise, can't we point that out and acknowledge them?

While I'm on the topic of testimonials there is a very easy way today to capture testimonials unlike less than 5 years ago. It brings the most credibility, sincerity, and candor from the client and is felt and seen from someone that is a prospective customer of yours. Today video cameras and video editing software are inexpensive, easy to use, and can be invaluable tools in your marketing strategies. Have you ever been to someone's website and they have written testimonials on their website, but they put John P. or Mary B., underneath the testimonials? Those may not seem credible to you.

Would you believe the testimonial of someone on video? Can you see sincerity on someone's face, hear their words, and believe what they're saying? This is much more convincing to me and I'm sure you feel the same way too. It's hard for someone to bluff on camera, unless they are professional actors. If the business is in your community, do you think that a person would risk their reputation by giving a false testimonial? Probably not as you will run into them at the supermarket, at your kids' school, or other community activities and chancing the risk of jeopardizing their political or social capital is not worth the risk.

## COMPANY WEBSITE

Do you have a company website that is not only a fancy brochure, but a place where your customers can come to get information that is valuable to them? A video testimonial can be a powerful tool to show your satisfied and elated customers who are there to bolster the position of your company and your credentials.

Almost everybody wants to be in front of the camera and be semi-famous. You customers should be proud of their decision to install solar and want to show off their system and how much energy and money it's saving their family or business. When you think about the investment to install solar, it does change people. It gives them back the power control more of their destiny. Capturing that emotion and experience through video on your website will inspire others to follow in their neighbor's footsteps. Haven't you ever been inspired in a similar way that caused you to make an important decision? We all have.

Is there a way on your website for your customers to access something like a calculator to prepare them and give them some sense of what it's going to cost to install solar at their home or business before they decide to call you? How about a lease payment calculator if they're not buying the system outright? Be creative and add more value to their online experience. This ties in again with the testimonial. If one of your neighbors has gone through this exercise and validated that they used the calculator on your website and it supports what they've purchased, how will that bolster their opinions about you? And what if they shared that it was accurate and the system is generating what the calculator said it will, do you think capturing a sentence or two about this in their video testimonial would encourage more customers to visit your website and validate you as a professional company that delivers on its promise?

Can you film an actual installation and show your customers very specific things that they might have questions about? One of the big items that's always the front of their minds is how the solar panels are attached to their roof. Remember they don't want any leaks and they also want to know that it is attached appropriately and looks sturdy. They also want to know, aesthetically, what the finished product will look like. You need to paint a vision for them as sometimes they can't see it for themselves. This vision doesn't stop at the residential level. Commercial and solar farm customers also want to see your work and visit projects to increase their comfort level with you.

In your video testimonial, can you ask a customer to show their before and after results a month or two later after your installation? This creates another level of credibility and perceived satisfaction from an existing customer in the eyes of the prospective customer who might be on the fence in deciding which service provider they're looking to go with. That connection will be felt or experienced in the future by the person visiting your website as they will see themselves experiencing those benefits.

# SOCIAL MEDIA

What online presence is working in the marketplace? Have you used Google ads, Facebook, LinkedIn, or Angie's List? As time evolves and technology changes, so will the methods for connecting with your prospects as well as creating raving fans of your brand and invariably your sales. Leveraging the Internet and all of its abilities to make you everywhere and available all the time will be a large part of your efforts to stay on top of your market. The Internet gives you a public relations platform to serve your customers' needs and maintain a progressive presence in the marketplace.

# CONTESTS

If you really want to draw some attention to your company, try a giveaway for a free solar system in the form of a sweepstakes or other contest. This will get you leads and also allow you to do detailed market research on what people are looking for when they're deciding to get the solar system. Forms can be created on your website that can be filled out very easily for the visiting public. A physical sign-up form will also be effective.

A contest can be tied in with your PR campaign and the announcement of the winner to create even more buzz. Being creative with contest rules can also attract people to sign up. You're only limited by your imagination and by your partnerships with the public and vendors, so don't be surprised by the interest of the public as they all want and need a solar system to reduce their homes electrical bill and would be inclined to sign up, because winning your prize is like winning the lottery.

# THE NEWSLETTER

Would you like to maintain your relationship with your customers long after they've made their purchase? If someone is visiting your website and they are a bit undecided but would like more information, would you like to provide something for them? This is where a newsletter can be automatically delivered to your customers by email on a frequency that you decide. The newsletter can include tips and tricks on how to save energy, the newest product offerings you have, your community involvement, and recent solar industry news and trends. It is a way to maintain a relationship with your existing customers as well as plant the seeds for your potential customers. Encourage them to share the newsletter with friends, families, and coworkers.

## CUSTOMER ACQUISITION COSTS

What are customer acquisition costs for a solar company? Sometimes I almost feel like it's better to be asking, what *aren't* customer acquisition costs for a solar company. To keep it simple, these are the costs associated with what you spend in order to have a customer to find you in the marketplace so they can do business with you. Often this is associated to what we would normally overgeneralize as marketing costs. Take the costs of all your marketing efforts—things like *Yellow Page* ads, newspaper ads, radio and TV ads, direct mail pieces—over the course of a prescribed period of time and divide them up by number of customers that you acquired over that period of time, and you would arrive at a baseline customer acquisition cost.

As earlier cited, quite conceivably you could hire independent contractors to sell for you and knock on doors all day, potentially eliminating some of your customer acquisition costs. You could potentially eliminate advertising and other forms of visibility in your marketplace, but is this what you want to do? Customer acquisition costs are part of doing business, but we all would like to reduce those costs as we know customers pay for everything. The less it costs us to find a customer and to do business with them, the more likely they're going to be interested in our products today and into the future.

Since I'm a big fan of examples, let's illustrate one here. Let's say you look at your marketing budget for the year and determine that you're going to spend your money across a few different areas as described in the previous paragraph. You invest money in a TV package, radio campaign, *Yellow Pages,* direct mail pieces and some newspaper ads. Your budget for all of these marketing strategies comes out to $50,000 for the year. At the end of the year you look at how many new customers you have, and in this example let's just say you acquired 100 new customers. This would mean that your customer acquisition costs to get those 100 new customers cost the company $500 each. This excludes any referrals, so track where your customers come from!

As we now see with many solar companies that are in hyper growth mode, they're usually spending a lot more than they probably believe to acquire new customers. We've seen some in marketplaces all over the country that are giving finder's fees of $500 to $1,500 just for referrals.

There are many different ways that people market their company's products and services today. All of those advertising and marketing activities need to be accounted for and realized as the true cost of offering your products and services. By not doing the math, you will be deceiving yourself into believing how much profit you're making at your company as there could be holes in your income statement in respect to your marketing budget and overall budget, which makes profits *appear* rosier than they actually are.

What I think I'd like to see in the industry today and the future is a new vision for how customers are traditionally acquired.

Referrals are not just the holy grail of growing your business, but when a referral is made, working with a potential customer becomes assisted buying versus selling.

If we go back to the earlier example of $50,000 a year for a marketing budget, would you rather acquire 100 new customers using a shotgun approach to marketing or give the money to an existing customer as a referral fee? This fee is not a bribe, so you can simply explain to them this idea that I just shared with you on how companies try so desperately to get new business, and the money always comes from the customer. You can reduce your customer acquisition costs and therefore reduce the costs of your services and become more competitive in the marketplace with less fixed costs.

Your approach to marketing is up to you, but remember that people want to do business with people that they like and trust. I know I said this in the sales chapter, but this idea is as old as Aristotle (or older). Often marketing with a shotgun to spread your name around is a knee-jerk reaction to scurry to acquire market share and visibility, but you won't know always know what is or what isn't working. It will often be very difficult to measure the results of the campaigns that you put in place and their effectiveness with this approach.

# CHAPTER FOURTEEN

# RISE ABOVE THE COMPETITION

How do you stand out and beat the competition in a crowded marketplace? Should you focus on price, value, relationships, or something else? The answer could be all the above or none of the above, so let's explore price, value, relationship, and perception. Getting a fair price, or the best price, for goods and services is a global mindset as well as a local mindset, but how we arrive at that number is complicated.

## PERCEPTION

Let's say two friends meet up that haven't seen each other in a while, and ironically the conversation drifts towards," I just had a solar system put on my house and you should come by and check it out"! They haven't spoken in a while and the other person also exclaims that they have had a solar system installed on their home. Now this is where the excitement begins, as it relates to price.

The next set of questions will usually be along the lines of, "What size of solar system did you get?" This is when the undertow of comparisons starts to creep into the dialogue; the conversation is leading up to, "How much did you pay for your system?"

Our human nature never wants to admit to another human that we may have paid too much for anything. I don't care if it's food, clothing, shelter, furniture, or automobiles. It's not something we like to acknowledge as it bruises our ego and often makes us appear gullible or an uneducated consumer. But here is where you can help the customer's ego for a second: comparing apples to apples, you must acknowledge that a solar system price can vary for many reasons. Each home can be unique, and the factors in their home compared to your home will allow everyone to "save face" because the variables that go into developing a selling price are custom for each solar system.

# COMMODITY

It's not like going to the auto dealership and deciding whether you want a white car or a silver car. The features and benefits of the car are the same, it only comes down to where you are going to buy it. Comparing the add-ons of the car is relatively straightforward because cars are mass produced in factories. Solar is made in a factory but your unique home and site conditions are not.

When you find yourself in a conversation about price comparisons, try to allow yourself to sit in the customer's position for a moment and think about how you offer your goods and services and do not just talk about price. Consider the other value-added services that you can incorporate into discussing the package so that price becomes less of a conversation piece.

From the viewpoint of the consumer, if both parties purchased a system within a reasonably close timeframe of each other, it should be safe to assume that price is similar. If they bought it from the same companies, then I would go out on a limb and say that most likely the price should be comparable. If both parties purchased their systems from different companies, pricing, features, and benefits can become hard to explain and distinguish. But to keep this a linear conversation, let's say that they used different companies but installed the same exact products for this example. For equal comparison we will also say that they both purchased their systems within the same calendar month.

In this story, the first person says they paid $3,000 less than the second person, and this is more than a 20% difference between the costs of the two systems.

# RIP OFF

Did the second person get ripped off by the company that installed their system? It would be hard to postulate without giving you more information, but this is where price and value intersect. To determine whether the second company is making more or less than the first company, you would really need to look deeper into the structure of their organization. It would be hard to understand, as we discussed in the chapter on developing a budget, what they need to break-even each day and what profit goals they have.

The first company might also be working out of their garage, have no marketing budget, and the owners' wife might be answering the phones and doing the bookkeeping, therefore reducing their baseline costs of doing business. They may also get better pricing for their goods, and their labor costs could be lower if the owner of the business is doing the installation.

Knowing all this I'm sure it's made you more confused than when you first started this chapter, but I wanted to give you some perspective that it can be unclear to a business and a consumer if price should be the determining factor in doing business. While you might be beating the competition on price, if you don't have a slush account to address unforeseen conditions, manage your budget, and create a strategy for growth, then the likelihood that you will still be in business will be left to luck. If you have a well-executed and continuously updated business plan, you can figure out how to rise above the competition.

# DIFFERENTIATION

Differentiation in the marketplace today will add value that is not just perceived but, most importantly, felt by your customers. People want to tell good stories about their great experiences with service providers. So how are you building rapport and increasing the "stickiness" of your brand in the eyes of your customers?

Back to those two people that we just spoke about in the beginning of this chapter. Once they learn that the other person has paid more, will they have a shift in perception? Most likely the person who paid more will be making a phone call, and your business has to be prepared for these types of calls. A customer who believes they paid pay 20% more than another customer will be bitter and offended, and they're going to want to know why.

Solar is not sold like a slice of pizza where everyone pays the same price regardless of their negotiating skills. Solar sales take into account a host of existing site conditions and variables that are often hard to quantify or justify as they relate to the final price. This should be communicated to your customer when this phone call happens, because it's usually not *if* but *when* the phone will ring. Even more insidious is no call and no referrals as a silent way of communicating dissatisfaction.

Perception becomes the new customer satisfaction survey, which is the reason for my insistence to contact each and every customer with a survey to get feedback on how you did. How can you shoulder this call with a clear and concise answer that will neutralize the customer's perceptions about you and your company? This is where you need to have a scripted or written down response that has been discussed with everyone in your company on how you serve your customers.

Each company will offer different services, whether it is 24/7 customer support or the ability to have a technician out the same day when there's problems, these services will help bolster your position when you are questioned on price. Your customer knows that solar systems are not maintenance free, and a solar system is a multi-thousand dollar investment that is projected to operate and last over 20 years. The same holds true for commercial and solar farm sized systems.

If it is a solar lease, the same rules apply. Be clear with the finance company of who will pay for service calls and how they will be handled. Know in advance and don't be caught by surprise. On the commercial side of the solar equation, the customers will also expect responsive service, and the price juxtapositioning is also intense as the system size gets larger and the price tag grows along with it. Adding value in the commercial and larger system sizes will come from a proven and deliverable track record. Companies that are interested in doing million dollar plus solar projects are going to want references and data points to decide who they're going to choose. For them, it's even more critical to have the maintenance program in place as the system size and energy output seems directly proportional the customers' expectations.

Did you ever think about offering a maintenance program, during the sales process? Do you come out to the customer's home, X times a year to clean the solar panels and to check other things about the system? Do you have an elite team of electricians who can do a home electrical inspection, provide a written report, and add value for many years into the future? Do you track the systems performance using web-based tools to ensure a long and productive system life?

# MAINTENANCE

How many solar companies do you know, that have said that solar is maintenance free? I know a few, and they say this because there are no moving parts, and with web-based monitoring solutions collecting data remotely has never been easier. But we know we need to maintain the system because, just like a car, after 5 years it's worked hard and has a lot of miles on it! We must take care of the customers' investment!

Over time, anything that's screwed or bolted together will become loosened with wind, temperature fluctuations, and basic expansion and contraction of the earth. Should penetrations on the roof be inspected periodically? You can answer these questions yourself and draw your own conclusions.

Some companies refute the need for maintenance because of the perceived hassle of having to service the customer after a large sale was made. They don't believe that they can make money servicing the customer in the future years, but part of their hesitation is that they did not have money built into the project for maintenance.

Do you remember earlier in this chapter when I spoke about price versus adding value? You do want to differentiate yourself in the marketplace, and this is one of the ways to do that. Do what others are not doing, and you will have customers that can depend upon you years into the future. This is not a marketing ploy, but relationship building.

This is where price starts to dissolve and value starts to appear. This new approach does require time, patience, training, commitment, and resiliency. I will touch on this briefly now, but I'd like you to think about your customer base when you're working on your exit strategy. If you had $X$ amount of customers on a maintenance program every year, you would have the opportunity to visit your customers 2 to 4 times a year. During these visits you could help them solve their problems as well as introduce them to new products that didn't even exist yesterday or the day you did your solar installation.

How else can I rise above the competition? Across the globe today, companies in the service sector, like solar, have to be truly service oriented. This means exceeding the expectations and anticipating your customers' needs before they even pick up the phone. If you tell your customer that it will take 3 days to install the system and you will start on the 15th of the month, meet or exceed what you promised them. Again, the human condition today wants its expectations to be exceeded and not be disappointed. If it's taking 5 days and you'll be there on the 20th, but haven't communicated this to your customer, how easy do you think it's going to be to get the next referral?

You might be thinking, what's the big deal? Well when you're dealing with residential solar, and we look at our society today, many families are dual income and have to be out working to support their families. If you scheduled your customer and they've taken the time off from work to be home and the schedule has changed, you've just cost them time and money. They might not say this, but they are now disappointed and can often carry a grudge around everywhere they go and share it with everyone they meet. We are an instant society: email, instant text messaging, access to the Internet, and information everywhere, all the time. Our expectations are higher than ever, and when they're not met, people will talk. What are they saying about your company? Hopefully only great things, but you need to work on your customer service game like a professional athlete, all the time.

Name bashing of other companies is a no-no, but if you're in business you must have an innate desire to compete. It's deep in our genetic makeup and that's what the framework of the Olympics is founded upon. So as you're "gladiating" in the marketplace today, how do you position yourself and your company and what happens when someone, like the customer, asks about another competing company?

# RUMOR HAS IT

How do you speak about your competition? Do you churn the rumor mill, point to their mistakes, discuss their unhappy customers, and express jealousy of their success? Get clear about who you are in the marketplace, and be conscious of what you say or don't say; your words will either open doors or get someone to not return a phone call.

Deciding how you feel and what you say about your competitors is entirely up to you. Often it can be construed as subjective either way, but ask yourself, what do you want people saying about you behind your back? It's perfectly natural to be proud of your company, your work, and your achievements, but complaining or grousing about the competitors can often be interpreted as having a "sore loser" mentality. My suggestion would be to focus on your customers and what your company is doing versus bad mouthing what others should be doing.

Customers will pick up on this immediately and it will reveal your level of sincerity and your authenticity. It's a very easy, knee-jerk reaction to put down a competitor, so take the high road and enjoy the view from above!

If we've added value at a reasonable price and own the relationship, the competition cannot get close to your prospective customer. If you don't have a strong relationship with your customers, you will be milked for your information and your proposal will be used as fodder for someone that has a better relationship. We all hate that in business, when we are first in to meet the prospective customer or we don't have that tight bond that we want to have with our prospective customer. This causes your proposal to be "shopped" and given to a competitor at times, or there is the propensity to have the customer tell your competitor what you quoted, as a cost per watt. Now you're on your heels, selling and competing on price, which is not the best position to be in.

By focusing on serving your community, your existing customers, and potential new customers, good things will invariably happen to you and your company. Sure there'll be times when you'll be tested and questioned on many things about your business, your staff, and the marketplace, but this is a very natural experience to have. It will always come down to what you're focused on. If the glass is half-empty, will always feel something is missing. If the glass is half-full, you will perceive plenty of work and abundance at your company.

# CHAPTER FIFTEEN

# SOLAR SUCCESS METRICS

When consulting with a company, I am often asked, "what are the key metrics that a solar company needs in order to be successful?" They are essentially the parameters involved to quantitatively assess, compare, or to track performance or production in any organization. With most businesses, there are very specific metrics that need to be tracked in order to understand the health of a company. Whether they are financial metrics, installation metrics, customer satisfaction metrics, or employee engagement statistics, we will highlight and show you what you need to focus on as an owner and also what you need to share with your management team to avoid many unnecessary surprises.

These all seem like big words but at the beginning of the day, there are certain metrics we should commit to memory. Committing to the metrics of your business is what turns a technician into a business person, but you don't have to have a business degree to track and understand metrics.

If you surveyed 100 solar companies today, 99 of them probably came from a technical background; they were either electricians or some other tradesperson. They could be an engineer or come from another specialized, degreed background, but generally they are not a business person by education. Business, as we know it, is generally not taught in schools, as I mentioned earlier in the book, and is not taught in union apprenticeship training programs. Unless you have decided pursue a business administration degree, or an MBA, a lot of these terms, or business metrics might be foreign to you.

This is why the typical contractor is usually making somewhere in the 3% net profit range. Tradespeople move up the ranks in a company and end up becoming business owners with very little understanding of business. Some of their mentors could be inappropriate role models for business but can teach them the technical aspects of the how-to do something with precision.

The other side of this is more deprecating. Suddenly, an employee can decide to leave their company and hang out their shingle to start their company with little or no business background. They have had no exposure to accounting or to understanding short- or long-term goals. This often is the beginning of the race to the bottom in a business.

There are quite a few solar metrics to track, so let's look at the ones that make the most impact in your business. We've already discussed customer acquisition costs, and this metric is very important. It's easy to look at the big picture but you need to get down into the weeds and know this metric as it can become prohibitively expensive to get customers and you might not be building this cost into your price of doing business.

# MAN-HOURS PER KILOWATT INSTALLED

How many man-hours does it take for your company to install one kilowatt of solar? This should be tracked religiously. Categorize the types of work you do into their own respective buckets. I recognize I gave you an example in the beginning of the book, but think deeper about this.

For example, if you're doing a lot of one-story, single-family residences that are 3 kW projects, track how many man-hours it takes to install these types of projects. Getting granular on site-specific projects and grouping them appropriately, will give you insight into more effectively managing your workforce, as you'll know how long they take to install. You will also give the team an incentive to complete projects and provide feedback when there has not been enough time allocated for tasks. This feedback is critical for a host of reasons. It will allow your sales manager and operations manager, if you have them, to be able to decide on taking certain projects. This helps if you need to keep everyone busy and working. You will have some room in your pricing structure in a competitive bidding environment, to decide to raise or lower your prices as you'll have a window into what those types of projects will take to do, time-wise.

This tracking can be done and should be categorized for the two specific scopes of work, which are electrical and mechanical work. Around the globe as well as on the factory floor, we like to call this *the division of labor*. The electrical work is self-explanatory, but what about the mechanical? Mechanical work usually means the things that are being mounted on a roof, like the attachments and the racking types of tasks. The division of labor is perhaps more clear on commercial projects and solar farms, but the ideas are the same. Chunk out the work by activities and tasks regardless of the type of work you do. By also knowing how long things take, on average you can get your field teams to be very goal oriented.

This might be new to your team and, like with all habits, will take time to cultivate. Some might suggest that there will be resistance to this metric, as it can be perceived as invasive. People have an intrinsic value to do well at your company and to perform. My sense is, historically you have never given your field people a schedule of values and broken it down in digestible chunks for them to understand. Traditionally they don't know what it takes or what the owner is thinking about when they are sent to a project to do an installation.

Part of this I believe is from fear that if we tell them all this information, they will then go out and start their own businesses and then we have essentially trained our competitors. But it's better for you and your business to be making money right now, while they're working for you, and not focus on the fear of them being your competition.

If they do decide to leave and start their own companies, isn't it better that they're educated and know what it takes to be in business because you've been transparent with them? At the very least, they're going to be tracking the same metrics that you are, and by sharing some of this business knowledge with them, they're going to know that they don't want to race to the bottom as well. If it seems counterintuitive to share, think about your aversion to it for as long as you have had it, sharing may just be the answer to a lot of your woes and culture challenges at your company. Remember, perception becomes the reality.

# GROSS MARGINS

This again is a good metric to follow but that needs to be backed up with tracking labor, tracking material costs, and effectively managing the overhead that would be allocated to the specific project. Gross margin talk is like bragging about how many millions of dollars in sales you did the previous year. It's great to talk about, but I'd rather focus on net profits. Gross margins can be about as important as the check engine light coming on; it's an indicator, but there's more to the light, and the information behind.

Are your margins 40%, 30%, 20%, 15% or do you know? Often when I ask this question to clients the answer can vary tremendously. This could be because we have seen the product cycles for solar spiral downward, specifically as it relates to solar modules costs, which today represents the largest percentage of a project cost. This can and will influence pricing strategies that companies employ to gain market share and will also affect their beliefs on scaling their business to capture market share at the expense of profit margins.

It is healthy to say that everyone wants more business, but what are you sacrificing as a result? Robbing Peter to pay Paul is not the answer. Look to Wall Street for supporting evidence of this or General Motors. You don't have to be them. So while gross margins are an important signpost for success, they don't always tell the complete story and can be deceiving when you can say you made $X$ % gross margin. What did you actually keep when the project was completed? Are you "really" done with the project and do you know that you will have no call backs? Administratively, is all of the paperwork done for the project? These are the types of things that erode the net profits of the jobs and trickle down into the actual retained earnings of your company.

While I briefly talked about this earlier I want to bring this up again: The idea of *shared accountability* between sales and operations is and will be the forefront of retail solar sales in the future. For companies to get scale and to grow, they need to know that both of these teams are working closely together to solve the customers problems and are being simultaneously rewarded for execution. This will improve gross margins and ultimately net profits.

With many of the companies that I consult with, their fixation on millions of dollars in sales is fantastic, but we want to focus on profitable sales. Wouldn't it be better to have less sales, more profits, happier customers, and ultimately satisfied employees who are eager to come to work every day to get rewarded on excellence? Wouldn't this be less for you to manage? Could you see this being a benefit of not being the biggest company in your area, but being the best? I'm sure you're going to enjoy figuring out how to implement these strategies in your company. Once they are implemented, you will get out of the adult daycare business and truly have a roadmap where you can grow the business as opposed to refereeing problem children, and margins will improve naturally.

The idea and controversy surrounding gross margins can be a bit unnerving for the business person in you, but I want to talk about it and go deeper into how it impacts you in a measurable way. There are many of rules of thumb out in the marketplace that relate to solar and construction in general.

It can be said that installation work, like solar, is usually a 25% to 30% gross margin business where service repair work can be double that. You see this in the plumbing and HVAC businesses with the added benefit of those types of businesses being duress based. When the AC breaks in your home in the summer, you want it fixed ASAP. When your sink is overflowing with water into your kitchen, you want service now. Unfortunately solar usually does not have urgent service needs.

# BREAK-EVEN

Do you know what your break-even point is? Like with all businesses, you need to know when your costs and revenue are equal, on a daily basis. You don't need to look at it every hour of every day, and it will change when you hire more people or your overhead expenses increase. This is not a sexy metric; it's not something that gets a lot of attention or interest. However it does influence your desired net profit margin, as you can work backwards from your break-even point on your cost of labor in your total overhead costs.

When you get really good at knowing what your numbers are and can chunk down what your actual selling price is per hour, you can then extrapolate that to what it costs per day for your labor. This will give you the big picture for your lead people in your organization as they are carrying the burden of the overhead in your company. Your lead journey people in your company are the productive engine that will cover your overhead and give you the retained earnings you're looking to achieve for being in business in the first place.

# CUSTOMER SATISFACTION

How satisfied are your customers with your company? Are they raving fans of your company or arch enemies that spread rumors about your company and maybe even you? Measuring this metric can be relatively straightforward and easy today. Whether you are using a web-based solution or going old-school and mailing them something to fill out and mail back to you, the intent is to get customer engagement, which happens so little in our businesses. It usually only happens when there is a problem and then there is the "all hands on deck" meeting to solve a customer problem. Wouldn't it be better to anticipate the problems ahead of time by asking good questions?

You also need to determine if you and your team are being consistent in your approach to your customers. Are they being treated with dignity and respect? There must be a high level of communication with them to what's going on with their project and knowing that your team is on schedule.

When you have a company policy, procedure, or methodology that is being questioned by your customers, it offers you an incredible opportunity to evaluate the standards of your company, as well as the people that you have chosen to surround yourself with. There are so many invaluable insights that your customers want to tell you, but you need to provide them with an easy way to do this. Everybody loves feedback and acknowledgment. Of course we don't want to be called at dinnertime when we're sitting down with our families, but there are other ways to reach your customers to solicit feedback on their experiences working with us.

If you need to provide compensation for doing this, then this looks like a bribe and I would not suggest this. Focus on areas that they believe, as consumers of your services, they would've liked to have seen or done better. Your company is humble and always looking for ways to add value and to serve your customers, and finding ways that they want to be serviced needs to be asked!

Mediocre service today is often just tolerated because everyone can blame that we're just being too busy to deal with anything. Do you settle for mediocre service? Do not neglect your existing customers, they have valuable information that you can use as metrics and that 90% of the other companies are not paying attention to.

# THE LIFETIME VALUE OF YOUR CUSTOMER

Do you know what your customers are worth? This metric can be hard to calculate if you are just doing installations and getting paid for them. Are there opportunities to own some of these solar assets in the form of power purchase agreements or leasing. So instead of having a customer pay for a system, in full and up front, they finance the system over time in the form of pay-for-performance types of arrangements, like power purchase agreements or monthly lease payments that are fixed.

Power purchase agreements are a vehicle where you, the owner of the system, are obligated and highly incentivized to maintain the solar system for the life of the contract because you will be paid based upon the performance and production of the system over its lifecycle. The benefit to the customer is that they usually enter into a long-term relationship to purchase power from the system at a fixed rate or a fixed rate with an escalator that usually tracks inflation or some other metric.

Leasing, on the other hand, is usually for a fixed fee per month and is not dependent upon performance but is based on an estimated calculation that the owner of the system and the customer, who usually becomes the host, agree upon in advance. However, if the system does not perform as contracted, usually there is compensation given to the customer.

What does all this have to do with the lifetime value of your customer? If you are just selling solar systems and are *not* entering into ownership relationships with your customer base, then the lifetime value of your existing customer that you just install the system for is close to zero. This is if you have not offered them a maintenance agreement or any other kind of way to continue your business relationship with them.

Quite simply, you sold them one item, albeit a large one, and probably will never communicate with your customer again unless there is a problem and they call you. Yes they can be a source of referrals, but that is another topic altogether. When you, as a business, become the owner of the solar system and enter into a contractual relationship with the host that's going to be using the electricity that is produced from the solar system, you now can start to look at the metric of lifetime value of your customer.

You'll be probably sending them a bill every month, so you'll be able to have a longer-term relationship with your customer in which you could offer other value-added services to them. Whether it's is a breakthrough for a new technology or another service that you're providing all of your customers, you now have an additional opportunity to serve them with your new offerings.

Most construction-related businesses, like solar, usually do not have lifetime value. Unlike a dentist, for example, who knows that you'll go to them over 20 years and the average revenue that they will generate every year are two annual cleanings plus other wonderful things like cavities and root canals. They can extrapolate this data to come up with the lifetime value of you in their chair. These metrics are used whenever a dentist wants to retire because they can show that they have potentially hundreds or thousands of people as their customers in their database. These customers all have a value to a new dentist just getting out of school and starting their practice or an established dentist in the same neighborhood that is looking for more customers.

# CHAPTER SIXTEEN

# THE TEAM: THINK SPORTS

Who are the people on your team at your company? If you are just starting out it might be you and someone part-time helping you answer the phones, doing bookkeeping, paying bills, and keeping things scheduled. You might have an apprentice that helps you on the job sites to get things done. Maybe you've grown a little bit beyond this and hired a journeyman to assist you with installations while your business is growing and you are getting more referrals and you can't be on the job each and every day.

## THE EARLY DAYS

Many businesses start out and develop a good reputation, are responsive, are well-liked in the community, and do good quality work. Like in many startups, from your garage to Silicon Valley, these are the halcyon days when you are immersed in the day to day stuff and wearing multiple hats.

Now your company has grown and you have a team, so who should you hire first for your next layer of the company? What other people, you could work with, whether they are directly employees or partners like we spoke about the previously. Are there tasks that you could outsource until you start making more money to justify the salaries, benefits, and other costs associated to their employment with you?

# SYSTEMS

I would focus on business development with a simple caveat: that you have a good system or framework for training the salesperson. It's also essential to have the ability to verify and check their assumptions about a project to confirm that a project can be done in the way that they're proposing it to a prospective new customer.

For many new businesses, this approach often comes with consternation and lots of deliberation. Will this person fit in and share the same values as I do? Will they represent our company the way we believe it should be represented? Are they just focused on their commission as a short-term goal or are they interested in helping you grow your business and will they be with you for the long haul? These questions will always haunt new businesses as well as established businesses in the solar field or any business for that matter. Business development or sales is a risk-reward quotient that is necessary for your business to grow and thrive. Picking the right people requires a little bit of science, a little bit of art, and, sometimes, a lot of grace or luck.

While I'm on this topic, and we're concerned about longevity of a new hire, think about this. Whether it's a salesperson or for any person in your company, let me inject an idea and thought that might invigorate you to look at teamwork again.

# NEXT HIRE

Let's revisit what type of company you have to determine your next hire. Is it more of a sales and marketing organization, are you a contracting entity, or do you provide both of these services under one umbrella? If you are the electrical contractor or another tradesperson, having somebody with great organizational skills would probably be a good candidate for the next person you should hire. This hire would be after the salesperson, unless you are going to assume this role. Yes they can still be like you, an electrician, but you need to think of this one basic tenet: how do you remove yourself from the field so you can focus on running your business as opposed to the business running you?

So in my example here, if it needs to be an electrician that shares the same values as you, but still needs some technical help as it relates to the solar industry, then send them for training. This investment in them will pay dividends long into the future and they'll really appreciate it. You'll also be able to get out of the truck and focus more on strategy. This isn't to say that you are walking away from your business and do not care about what happens in the field, but you can go out and inspect their work to increase your comfort. With today's technology on our phones and tablet computers, they could quite easily take photos or small videos of the work they've performed to increase your comfort on their skills and ability. This saves you a trip in the car and the old saying is true that time is money.

In many ways this type of documenting is a good idea anyway, so you can create the framework for how installations are done and archive this data to be used as training material for new hires. Document how you want projects done, visually. Most installation types of people and even salespeople use pictures to help understand the technology as well as instill what is possible to do at a site and what isn't.

If you are coming from outside the electrical contracting business, then my first suggestion would be to partner with an electrical contracting firm that has the requisite licenses that are necessary in that jurisdiction in order to perform electrical work and do your solar installations for you.

# I'M NOT A SALESPERSON

Many electrical contractors or ex-electricians have not been exposed to sales and marketing as much as you may have been. They are often quite content with just doing installations as many of them will claim that they are "artists or craftsman" and enjoy doing this more than "selling." They have been exposed to "bidding jobs," but this is much different than selling, as price usually dictates whether or not they will have work in a bidding environment.

I've found across the country today that these types of partnerships not only work but are mutually beneficial. Everyone gets to have their role and function and do what they enjoy doing and or excel at. I touched on this earlier, but I like to reinforce that you understand to do what you do best and comes what naturally to you and empower an employee to do what you don't enjoy doing. The same holds true for partnering: find people or companies that are good at what they do and you can get out of the way!

If you are coming from outside of the electrical contracting business, who is your first new hire? If you are a contractor, but not an electrical contractor, partnering with an electrical contractor would work well. They are looking for more work and they want to keep their own people busy in their company, and they usually welcome more of what they love to do, installation work.

If you are a roofing contractor you probably want to hire additional salespeople if you don't have them already as well as a project coordinator that can assist and be the liaison between the electrical contractor, the customer, and any vendor relationships. Depending upon the type of business you currently have and the one you want to have, there are a lot of ways to get there from here.

Hiring staff or partnering can work in either case. But if you still feel the need to keep the work in-house, then you need to determine what part of the supply chain you want to be in. Know the roles and functions and the capabilities of your current team and support their strengths and then find people that can fulfill weak areas in your company. Until your company has more work than it knows what to do with, I'd advise partnering with engineering firms, electrical contracting firms, roofing firms, etc.

Think of your solar company like a general contracting company. Specializing in the beginning is the key to not getting too big too fast and being able to manage overhead costs while keeping everyone busy. Sometimes we want to control everything and simultaneously, we control nothing. You need to hire and surround yourself with very smart people that are willing to work hard to serve your customers. They should simultaneously understand the competitive landscape while holding a vision for the future in regard to the direction you are going with your company.

Look at any professional sports team: baseball, basketball, or football and see how these franchises work to attract the most talented people to their organizations, and remember the influence that they have on their customers or fans. The metaphors are the same for your business. Who are you going to attract to your organization and who do you think is going to go to the World Series?

# CHAPTER SEVENTEEN

# COMPENSATION STRATEGIES

The question about hiring and compensation requires you to look at current market conditions in your area. This would be the first step but not the last. Back to my sports analogy, sometimes you have to pay more than any other team to get the best players if you want to win the Super Bowl. Paying for talent isn't anything new. It happens in corporate America each and every day as well as in small businesses across the globe. But you still need to gauge your people to determine pay: consider their skills, education, attitude, and work ethic.

Look at compensation and set it up into multiple buckets. The first framework is obviously the base salary or an hourly compensation plan. Second, look at the basket of benefits: the paid time off, vacation time, paid sick leave, paid training, and some form of retirement package as the foundation of your compensation structure.

The next step would be to look at incentivizing your team based upon their sphere of influence as it relates to the metrics that are important and that they have control over. If it's a journeyman electrician, as an example, they have influence over labor productivity or effectiveness as it relates to the planning and installation of a solar project. You need to breakdown a project's tasks for them so that they can understand and have influence over these decisions as well as buy-in, which psychologically is most important in influencing change of old habits and gives them new goals.

# SMART

Goals have to be specific, measurable, attainable, realistic, and timely (SMART). If they hit the milestones set out for them, and these can be measured at the end of a project, you now have a new dialogue to reference. However small a project is, keep score and make the information available to your team. At the end of projects, sit down with them so they can actually have some input, feedback, and influence on that project as well as projects in the future.

One of the ways that they could be compensated is based upon our earlier discussion about sold days. If they are out on the projects and consistently executing, meaning they are hitting their man-hour per kilowatt goals or meeting or beating budgeted hours against the actual hours, then there is a clear and measurable way to see their performance and their effectiveness. Yes there will have to be rules around the criteria for additional compensation, but this does not have to be very complicated to explain and implement. If we base compensation on the sold day and we cover our overhead in 16 of the 21 days in the month, then we should reward them for execution as we've covered our overhead at our company.

You can see how aligning the goals of the company and the goals of the field people can be easily attained with information and feedback. They know what a day of work is and we we've already explained to them what we expect of them. If there is a deviation from the onset, we will know because they will know that it will influence their compensation and impact not just themselves but also their other team members.

When a group is going to suffer, as a result of an individual's actions, an amazing thing happens. Peer pressure starts to influence the decision-making process in one of two ways. First, decisions that are made lean towards the group when the individual knows the choices they make will effect the group. The second thing that happens is when an individual doesn't consider the impact of the group, the individual gets feedback from the group and often it is the catalyst to work as a team, or go work on another team at another organization. Powerful motivators at work here!

Just a point of clarification, it is not to suggest that everyone comes to work seeking additional compensation for the sake of being, what could be described as "money hungry." What I'm driving at here is if every journeyman in your company is compensated at the exact same pay, this new pay structure establishes a few very important and significant cultural shifts and brings out a very positive competitive nature in people. It will show everyone on the team that if you work hard and reach the mutually agreed upon goals, which are easily understood and clearly attainable, we will recognize you and reward for performance.

I want to emphasize that compensation doesn't have to come in the form of money alone. Some people would be very happy with acknowledgment to additional time off. The key to all this is to sit down with your team on an individual basis and ask them what they want. Some want the money, some want other things. It's your responsibility to ask these questions and wait for their responses. I can assure you that some of their responses will surprise you.

Could you see how this could revolutionize how you do business today and how it could reshape the goals of everyone? Do you think anything would be different at your company if you retooled and rewired everyone's current way of looking at how business is done? The benefits are immeasurable and this ties in directly with shared accountability in your organization.

What are the other benefits to your employees of compensation based upon performance? Well for starters, how about your team understands that throughout the year they can make more money based upon their influence and not just yours. Employees are usually waiting towards the end of the year for that ubiquitous year-end bonus. Sometimes, what happens is that the first 8 months of the year, the employees' performance has been exceptional. Through faults or no fault of their own, they have a difficult fourth quarter. When you are getting ready to assess someone's performance, as in this instance, what really sticks in your mind the most? Was it the first 8 months or the last quarter? This can have a lot of unintended negative consequences for both you and your employee. It makes both parties in the relationship uncomfortable, which is why you should pay for performance all year long.

# PERFORMANCE PAY

You can see why the concept and practical application of paying for performance throughout the year gives everyone immediate feedback and recognition that might be lost under the usual framework of the year-end bonus.

One of the other great benefits that is often hidden comes from my own personal story. You have your year-end party where your employees and their spouses and family come. People start fraternizing and talking about the year. Suddenly one of your employee's spouses comes up and asks the fateful question, "How come so-and-so received their bonus in August?"

That's a great question for a couple of reasons. First, it shows, in this instance, a spouse that is paying attention to the income received as a result of their spouse's performance at your company. Second, they understand that the culture in your company is one of performance and teamwork. Third, which ties in to answer the spouse's question, which I had to answer one year and my response was, "Why don't you ask your spouse?" I think by saying this they understood what I was getting at for the most part. Excluding outside influences, if set up correctly, your team will know how to perform, what is expected of them, know the rules of engagement, and be able to influence the outcome. So, the employees know each day, week, and month how they can influence their performance pay and I'm confident this information trickles into the employee's home, as usually their spouses see the paychecks and the accompanying pay stub, outlining what their compensation was for that pay period.

Another distinct thing happens when these types of programs are implemented in your company. Human nature kicks in— people talk! What I'm driving at here is that just as owners talk, salespeople talk, and so do others at all levels of your organization. They talk to other people at other companies who would be characterized as their equals. They all ask things like compensation structure, benefits, and culture and so on to get a sense of what it's really like to work for you or what it's like working at other comparable companies in the same business sector.

Perhaps this type of talk could lead to a recruiting opportunity. When recruiting talented people to your company doesn't it make sense to be a little different and implement some of strategies that will have a long-lasting effect on not just your company but also will have an effect on the families of your employees as well as, potentially, the industry itself?

Are you comfortable with making a difference and making a fortune at the same time? The statement might seem bold to you, but I think it will always come down to, are we as business owners "willing or able" to make a shift in how people are not only compensated but also recognized for their valuable contributions. We can see in the statistics across our country that performance, if not managed effectively, eliminates industries overnight. This is part of what I like to characterize as retraining America and the world for business today and in the future.

When I say to people, "You have a great attitude, you're hired" I get the look like people have been immobilized or have seen a ghost. How does a great attitude fit into my company? It can be said that positive people with great attitudes are truly infectious while people with less than positive attitudes and who are difficult to work with become layers of distractions throughout your entire organization.

We've all worked where somebody is very difficult to work with and everyone seems to be talking about this person at the water cooler. You can only imagine for a second how much time and energy is being expended by focusing on someone that might not be a good fit for your organization. What does this cost the company?

Conversely, someone can be hired that is a delight to work with, is eager to learn, and does not get frustrated very easily. They are determined to figure out whatever is put in front of them. They come to work early and stay late. They stop to help people just because they're asked. Customers are enthusiastic about them and let you know about it. Don't you want more of them in your orbit?

We have all either called a place of business or visited a company and have been impressed with someone's enthusiasm and personality over the phone or when we are first greeted at a company. It sets the tone, doesn't it? It starts to shape your opinions, whether you like it or not, about how you feel or think about doing business with them.

The next question you need to ask yourself then, is it better to hire for attitude or to hire for skill? We all know that we can train for skill if they have the aptitude, but can we train for attitude? You can decide this for yourself but I think you know the answer. We have all made mistakes in hiring in the past. Whether we were mesmerized by a masterfully crafted resume that resembled a super person or someone was exemplary in the art of interviewing, we have got it wrong more than once and if history is any indicator, the likelihood of this occurring again has a high probability.

When someone is applying for employment at your company and they have a well-polished resume with lots of references and perceived longevity (meaning they have been employed for long periods of time with just a few companies), what can you say to them? What I suggest you do is a little unusual, but ask them how they're going to contribute to the company. You should want to know how they can improve the condition of the company. Notice I didn't say to ask them, "tell me about your credentials, tell me about your certifications" and so forth. Those things should already have been considered prior to you talking to them. What you want to know, which ties together with attitude, is how someone is going to join the company and make a difference by contributing.

Contribution, as you can quite imagine can come in many forms. Could you see how compensation can be affected by the correlation between selection, attitude, training, and skills? Having the greatest sales compensation plan will do nothing for the profitability and culture of your company if the values of the people installing the systems are not equal and in alignment.

I will always suggest getting the framework set up right from the start, and this is a basic tenet that I'm describing that can be tested through time as human nature meets a new paradigm for business today. Compensation structures or plans for administrative people seem to be the hardest to blueprint. Rewarding your accountant or bookkeeper on a performance metric like speed can be challenging because we really want them to be accurate and not "cook the books." We can still ask our accounting department for complete and accurate financial statements by the tenth of the month. This does require them to ask the other respective departments for timely submittals so that they can do their jobs effectively, and this requires a lot of teamwork and support as well as a very large undertaking of cooperation.

Other administrative staff that supports operations or sales could be also incentivized on performance. Whether they get a percentage of the overall group's activities is one way to structure this. Think about how they impact and influence positive outcome in the role and function that they serve, and keep in mind the people they support and develop a compensation structure that encourages repetition of good habits. If it comes down to simple things like reaching goals such as booking appointments or completing specific paperwork in an expeditious manner, then there are metrics to recognize their achievements and their contribution to the company so you can reward accordingly.

# DEFERRED COMPENSATION

By having a stake in the profitability of the company, you can see how your team's goals and your goals are more in alignment. Could you see how they would approach customer service or sales and operations like it was their own company. This happens at all publicly traded companies, and it happened when I sold my company. When people have skin in the game, they are more vested in the outcome. They know what is at stake and will usually put their best efforts forward for the sake of the whole company because they will benefit economically as well as in many other ways. We don't need to look very far by reading the newspapers in the business section or reading online to see how people can become newly minted millionaires by working at companies and receiving stock options.

Let me preface that it is not about becoming a millionaire: This is more about your team and having everyone's goals of serving your customers and being profitable at the forefront of everyone's mind. It allows everyone to contribute and have shared accountability in your company. In many small companies, another strategy would be an employee stock ownership plan (ESOP). Now I'm not a financial advisor so you can do your own research on this but the basic idea is the same: focus on results, not on activities, and reward accordingly.

Many small and medium-size companies might only utilize stock option plans for the founding or principal members of the company. Stock options often can be time-consuming and sometimes expensive to administer internally or they need an outside, third-party firm to administer the plan.

Again this is very similar to what happens in a publicly traded company and there are many resources on the Internet as well as through your local attorney and accountant that can help you structure plans that incentivize performance with all of the criteria set forth in documents that specifically outline how the compensation package works and what you need to do in order to redeem them.

While compensation strategies can vary across the globe, you need to consider one simple axiom: People will either want more money, more time off, or more recognition for their accomplishments. Most will choose money, as it seems many people never have enough of it. Some will argue for more time off. Either way, you need to understand that installing solar systems boils down to doing task work. This is connected directly with time. If someone can do more in less time, you will be more efficient and be able to share the wealth. It's a systems based approach to business that, in a competitive solar industry, is crucial to your longevity and sustainability.

# CHAPTER EIGHTEEN

# EXIT STRATEGY

I've gone through the due diligence process at the "Goldman Sachs level," and on through many levels of "deal heat" to the final day of closing and seeing the escrow check wire transferred into my bank account. It was exhilarating to experience, a true moment of achievement, but I knew there was more to life than the money, as there is always something new to learn, experience, and to ultimately make a difference, give back, contribute to and leave this place a little better than you found.

## THE END IS THE BEGINNING

The exit is really a new beginning, and I can tell you how you can set yourself up to get there from here. Whether you decide to never sell your company, or if you just want to create a roadmap to be able to do it, I recommend everybody should have the framework set up to at least be able to decide. Things change in our lives for many different reasons and being stuck with a business that is unsatisfying causes us to lose our passion for what we started in the beginning. If you started a business to achieve freedom, but can't be free, why stay in that business? This is obviously not the only reason why you started a business, but when I ask people why they did, they usually say that was one of the reasons.

There could be a whole book written on exit strategies and how to get there from here. They vary by industries, market conditions, buy-sell agreements, and the interests of both parties and sometimes even other suitors. How do you determine the value of your company? This question gets asked a lot in business by business people who are looking to sell what they believe is an asset to someone or a group that sees value in what they have created.

# VALUATION

While I'd love to tell you what your business is worth, I would be disingenuous to suggest this. Valuations can be all over the charts depending upon the buyer and the seller and what each of them wants as a result of the transaction and how the relationship will grow from that point. There are many business brokers in the marketplace today as well as websites and local attorneys that can guide you to determine what the valuation is of your business. I have given a lot of tips in this book to help you think about recurring revenue and other things of value that will make a potential suitor enthusiastic about acquiring your company from you.

If your business is strictly based upon doing contracting work and you have little or no pipeline of future work and you have little or no recurring revenue, the valuation of your company will surely be less than one that has multiple streams of revenue.

Some owners of businesses stay on during the transition to onboard the new company's brass in order to familiarize them with the company's operations and staff. I would recommend this for many reasons. If you kept the acquisition a secret from your people, they have now become surprised that the company has been sold and they'll want comfort in knowing that things will be ok and that they still have jobs.

Usually, for companies that are purchased, the owners are offered employment agreements to stay on and steer the ship through the new ocean with the new fleet at their side to support reaching mutual goals. Even in high-tech companies, we see this often. The principals are the founders of the companies and usually stay on board when companies come and acquire other companies. This approach is not just about material possessions but more about people that made it all possible.

Because it will always be about people and not about the widgets that the people make, especially in the solar business, companies are acquiring talent and positioning in the marketplace. This is not to say that a company was not acquired based on their widget or their intellectual property, but it really boils down to the humans: the individuals and team that made it all possible.

## COMPANY PROFILE

Sometimes you need to put yourself in the shoes of the companies that are looking to enter into your business and know what they're thinking about as it relates to buying a prospective company.

What are they really looking for?
What are the things that are important to them?

Is your customer base strong?
Can you offer other services to your customer base?
Do you have any recurring revenue?
Do you have positive cash flow?
Are you making money?

The list can go on but you should be thinking now about what your company has that other companies of similar caliber do not have and how you're different. They want to know what your solution is to the saturation problem of companies cloning themselves like yours in the marketplace and how you're dealing with these threats. What is your "secret sauce" and what could hamper your success?

Throughout this book I've tried to emphasize to you the importance of beginning with an end in mind, a.k.a. the exit strategy. Setting the framework up to win, does require work and potentially rewiring your brain a bit and how you look at your day-to-day company as well as the big picture. Getting the right people in the right positions is definitely part of it as it "takes a village" to run an effective company. This effort requires you to examine your own beliefs about what's possible and what is not in your business and in your life. The internal struggle that you could go through is similar to the caterpillar as it goes through its metamorphosis to become a butterfly. From crawling to flying, all the internal growth must occur in you. You will need the support of your family, friends, and coworkers to support you in reshaping your company and preparing for this endeavor.

# AUTOPILOT

What do companies look for when they are thinking about buying you and your company? At its very core, they are looking for competent people that operate well-run businesses. One of the hallmarks of this is a company that runs when the owner is not there. The company should have developed systems, procedures, policies, and directives for all the roles and functions within their structure. Some business owners can take a few days off, and for others it means they could be gone for 2 weeks to a month, and things would be the same when they got back.

Perform this self-assessment. Could your company operate without you for more than a few days, weeks, or months? This is the first part of the journey of evaluating your current situation and you have to find the courage and strength to acknowledge if you do not have systems in place. The people and processes must be prepared in order for you to step away on your terms. Developing systems and layers of management requires you to trust in their decisions and rely on the systems to work when you aren't there.

# GROWTH

When evaluating businesses, potential suitors are also looking for growth potential in the marketplace. They are determining if buying your company will allow them to reduce barrier time to entry. Starting a new company would be very expensive and time-consuming, or they could buy your company and leverage your hard work and avoid the start-up syndrome.

This is why acquisitions are probably the most desirable way for companies to get scale and grow beyond the organic way that they have been growing since their inception. Larger organizations that have lots of working capital and zero cash flow problems, as well as great relationships with lending institutions and are ideally positioned to make great offers to companies like yours. They will look for a strong management team, solid accounting history, flexible relationships with banks and a good reputation in your marketplace so it would be helpful to get prepared if an acquisition is something you are interested in.

Many people that read this are probably saying that they will never sell their companies and want to "go at it alone." What I mean by "going at it alone" is simply that they want to do everything and they believe that no one can do it better than themselves. When control is all in the owner's hands, their ability to delegate or to let the people they've hired do their jobs gets interrupted. The owner's inability to relinquish control of every decision creates obstacles that can greatly hinder the success of a company. They can believe that even the very people they hired are not good enough to be instructed if they were tasked to do the basic activities associated with the day-to-day work of installing solar.

Just to clarify, it's not just the solar industry but many more businesses across the globe that are inflicted with this malady. It seems like a lot of this stems from the simple fact that they've never been exposed to a system or framework that allows someone to segue from being a technician to a business person. This applies to the broadest range of tradespeople, from solar to a shoemaker.

You either have a good peer group and learn new things or have an old reference point on how things are done that might not be serving you well. Many small business people lack this exposure causing them to have a reference point that is myopic and potentially outdated. Most people in the solar business have trade associations, but small business people often lack a personal board of directors that they can bounce things off of and get CEO-to-CEO guidance. Find a group that is better at business than you are and be mentored.

This is why I believe that the cliché of "it's lonely at the top" holds true, because when you have no one to mentor you or show you things from a different perspective, you can certainly feel alone.

# FREEDOM

It's kind of ironic, that people start businesses to have more freedom, more time with their families and doing the things they love, when often the opposite happens. They don't trust anyone to fulfill new and existing customers' needs as they believe they are the only ones that are suited for this. While I respect the independent operator, as at one time I was also in that situation, it disturbed me immensely that I was working Monday through Sunday, 24/7/365 with very little time off to do the things that really mattered outside of the workplace. I questioned my decisions to go into business, and my saving grace was that I was humble enough to look for answers.

Giving up control to anyone or to any entity is something that many are unwilling to negotiate. To those people, I say as long as you're going to go at it alone, you had better charge the right price for your products and services and save money for your retirement. Make time for your family and hobbies and do the things you love, because there will be a time when you're ready to retire and you won't want to climb the ladder anymore. Regardless of this, I still want to see you successful, so follow the information in this book to give you the tools, resources, strategies, and tactics to have a compelling future.

# CHAPTER NINETEEN

# BOLD PREDICTIONS

Solar is a disruptive technology for power generation, and the traditional, centralized power plant architecture will change incrementally as solar growth will continue to seep into the infrastructure for a host of reasons. When we talk about changing the landscape, we look at a host of factors contributing to the shift.

## CODA

The levelized cost of energy (LCOE) from solar is becoming on par or less than traditional methods of energy generation, from nuke, natural gas, oil, and coal. This shift will encourage and foster more people and businesses to segue to clean energy than ever before in our history for purely economic reasons alone. Externalities—what it truly costs for existing power generation and their impacts—will be more relevant. Look to the Japan Tsunami aftermath or commodity prices as cues to the shift in consciousness, both personal and political, which will further invite alternative forms of power generation to the grid.

The idea of the cheapest source of energy will not be the only deciding factor for citizens when selecting how they will use energy around the globe. Solar has enjoyed an accelerated decrease in manufacturing costs and more innovation on areas surrounding the solar panel: inverters, installation methodologies, performance measuring and monitoring, codes and standards, utility adoption, and government red tape is being reduced. All of these factors will contribute to wide-spread adoption of the technology as it's within reach more and more each day for consumers. In developing nations, this will also become accelerated, as the cost to bring in power to remote areas will be displaced with deployable and reliable solar technologies and energy efficiency that was economically unaffordable less than 5 years ago. The tipping point for current energy pricing has influenced homeowners and businesses as to how they gain control over a variable cost and then fix that cost utilizing solar technology as well as other supporting technologies that work hand-in-hand with a solar system.

I can make a few other predictions for the coming years that might seem far-reaching today, like looking at a *Popular Science* magazine from 30 years ago and being shocked at what they printed then and what came to fruition today.

# STORAGE

Storage is going to be the holy grail of energy as we know it. Combining self-generation with a storage technology will allow people to flee the grid en-masse. Some will form co-ops and their own independent and relatively small power companies and snip the wires from the utility and become their own mini utilities. The ability to finance these types of decisions will be as simple as signing up for a mortgage type of product or some other financial arrangement and working with a service provider that has morphed into a utility-like company, with entrepreneurial traits associated to their corporate governance and their desire to serve their communities and customers.

Accessible storage that is affordable for residential consumers will create the next Microsoft or oil baron type of company if partnered with the right technology, leadership, and financing. Energy is the largest business in the world, and creating suitable storage for the energy generated by a homeowner or business will revolutionize the world energy stage as we know it.

When storage becomes developed in a scalable way, the threat to utilities will be felt and they could someday be left with transmission and distribution, rather than production, as their business model. These traditional utilities will hope to create unregulated subsidiaries to shore up their balance sheets and be competitive as they will have stranded assets that need to be paid for that could not be fully amortized. This will happen in areas of high electricity rates first and slowly spread elsewhere as entrepreneurs and their ideas will meet the marketplace. There could also be partnerships with the existing utilities and these entrepreneurs to dovetail their strategies, as local public utility commissions across the globe will receive increased pressure from rate payers for relief from high and unpredictable energy costs.

# SOLAR PANELS

Solar panels will incorporate AC output built right into them. Just like any other appliance that essentially has a cord on them, they will truly become plug and play. Currently this is done bridging two separate components: a solar panel and a micro inverter. By combining the two at the manufacturing level, you reduce the embedded costs associated with bringing both products to market and also reduce the installation costs.

# FINANCING ENERGY

You may have heard of Software as a Service (SaaS) Model for software as well as power purchase agreements (PPAs) or Lease programs for solar. Well this will evolve for storage in a big way. Financial institutions will embrace this for a multitude of reasons, including the certainty that people will need energy 24/7/365. The financial institutions could reduce the risks on their balance sheets and secure a source of recurring revenue through energy financing.

Solar will be as ubiquitous as an appliance that can be picked up at the local big box retailer. It will be simplified to a point where heavy engineering calculations will be predesigned into the architecture and software will assist in managing the interaction with the grid. Your home will be an energy generation source, and a battery of some kind will be used to assist everyone that is on the grid in power management, if you choose to stay on the grid. Perhaps there will be incentives for you to be connected to the grid for stability and support (although I'm less bullish about this one).

Lastly, we will see people in homes and businesses go "off grid" just as we've seen telephones go from wired to the mobile platforms we see today. There will be great business models around this, as the 24/7/365 need to deliver power at an affordable and predictable way will change how we look at the energy distribution of the last 100 years.

# SUBSIDIES

The training wheels will come off the solar industry and the need for subsidies will be a thing of the past. This will happen for a few reasons. First, the costs of the products like the solar modules and the innovation to drive down the remaining balance of system components will be on par with the current prices we already pay for energy. Second, more projects will use financing as a vehicle, as previously outlined. This will be combined with a higher level of accountability in our industry that we see now: paying for the energy produced. We see this across the globe in the form of feed-in-tariffs and renewable energy credits. Connecting performance and production to a solar power plant will raise the bar in the industry and wean us off of tax credits in lieu of production-based incentives.

# WINNERS AND LOSERS

As with all businesses that evolve, there will be a slew of winners and losers. Picking them is a challenge, but there are symptoms and visions for the future that are hard to ignore. On the winning side you will see storage take the lead. My take is it will be not very obvious today but within the next 5 years we will be as surprised as we are with the evolution of mobile phones. Large industrial companies will own these storage assets and deploy them strategically to support the grid via the utilities and eventually create their own utilities or micro grids.

# CAPITAL MARKETS

While not much support has come out of the financial system since its teetering on the brink of a second great depression, I believe that lending institutions and the capital markets will bring much-needed investment into the solar energy space. The banks know it's the largest market in world energy, so they will continually plow money into research and development of renewable energy. Picking the next winners won't be easy, but like a roulette table, they will spread their chips all over the board.

We will also see crowd sourcing of financing renewables and the potential for legislation to change master limited partnerships, which will work like a stock fund that is a liquid asset to own. Bond funds can also be a vehicle for an investment instrument. People want to invest in solar, like a stock or mutual or index fund. The companies that have the best assets and are performing optimally will be able to provide a stable rate of return for their investors. This happens now, but usually at the tax equity level of large banks and insurance companies. It will go from Wall Street to Main Street allowing citizens to invest in each other.

# CHOICES

While this seems obvious, let me explain. In most markets across the face of the earth, we use commodities to be the feedstock of the energy source that gives you light, power, heating and cooling, and other forms of convenience that we often take for granted. By finding and using renewable energy and paring it up with storage, every citizen of every nation will be able to manage their variable costs for electricity and turn them into fixed costs. It's kind of like signing a 30-year fixed mortgage for your home versus a 5 year or a perpetual balloon payment. The extra or discretionary income will further bolster our economy and fuel more innovation with energy and create more jobs.

Today, as of this writing, the manufacturers of solar modules are experiencing significant pain financially due to oversupply and commoditization of the space, whereas a few short years ago, their position was very different. Like the tech industry, if a product can be manufactured globally, the pricing power will decrease precipitously over time, like Moore's law with computers. There will be consolidation in the solar panel manufacturing space, as large multi-national companies will have the strong balance sheets to spread these costs across their companies. They will also have the added benefit of spearheading innovation and improving upon the current technology platforms we see in the marketplace.

# CONCLUSION

It's clear to me that solar will revolutionize how we will use energy well into the future and coupling it with new storage technologies will be at the forefront of these discoveries. But before we get too excited about what is coming, let's look at where you are at now. The solar success principles outlined in this book will be the framework for you to grow your business and road map in tandem, how you want to live your life outside of the four walls of work.

A lot of different perspectives surround what we are calling today, the *green movement*. Some may have been typecast in previous years as being hippy culture, but the world has changed its representation of this, as "green" is not only here to stay, but a way of life for corporate culture as well as your community.

The opportunities are immense. The trillions of dollars in positive benefits to our global economy impact more than energy, but also food, water, and other resources that we can often take for granted. Deciding how you are going to be part of this way of life is your choosing. Whether its directly related to solar, energy efficiency, advocacy, engineering, finance, or construction, there has never been a more appropriate time in history for you to help, and your contribution is vital to our shift in how our energy economy evolves.

My intent for you in reading this book is multifold. It was written with you, the small business person, in mind. If you follow the Bureau of Labor Statistics, you know that small business is defined as companies with less than 500 employees, and those companies represent 99.7% of all firms in the United States. The statistics are staggering as to how many small businesses struggle economically. A lot of this has to do with the lack of resources for developing a framework of systems and accountability, as most businesses are way too busy putting out fires in their companies and spend a majority of their time reacting to the daily events and have little time to implement any planning into their long-term strategies. So apply the knowledge of this book and enjoy the results, as so many tangible and intangible benefits to you and to society as a whole.

The information and principles contained in this book are the blueprints for the success for your solar company. You can take out *solar* as the title and industry and replace it with whatever you'd like. Any business that sells their time and might sell some product, which is summarized as selling labor and materials, can benefit immensely from the information here. The basics such as budgeting, building your sales and field teams, marketing, and customer service are all embodied in this book.

I will be the first one to confess that if you believe that money is going to light you up, you're in for a world of hurt. Sure even the monks at the monastery would like to have more money to feed their flocks, but there will always be more reward in serving others. The many faces of our society from the mainstream media, Hollywood, and keeping up with the Jones' have led us to believe that money is the answer. We have been led to believe it will solve all of our problems, but when if you look at people that have lots of money, often it can be the root of all their problems.

If you're struggling in your business and you get some morsels of wisdom out of this book, apply what you've learned and stay focused. Yes, there'll be many people that will discourage you from taking the road less traveled. If I listened to people saying it can't be done, you would not be reading this book. Surround yourself with positive people that will foster and encourage you. Other people's fear should not extinguish your desire to get to the strategies, methods, people, and systems that can improve the quality of your company and your life. I suggest to everyone to evaluate their peer group from time to time, especially when someone tells you, that "you can't do it or it's impossible."

I'm living proof that anything is possible if you have the drive, hunger, passion, and desire to serve. If you take the time and apply this information in a very simple and understandable way in your company today, you'll start to see changes, not only in your financial results but in the culture of your organization.

What I've seen from other companies as a result of implementing these strategies has been revolutionary. Just as you go through your own personal and professional metamorphosis, so will your employees. Some will take to this as a new beginning and be excited for everyone involved, while others will resist this like the black plague. There will be people that will be resistant to this change because they were comfortable with less shared accountability.

If what are you doing today is a constant source of frustration and you are not getting the desired results you know you can, I'd encourage you to apply the information in this book, if not just for your company, but for yourself and your family. The change has to begin with you and I've laid out a map for you to achieve that, but I can't come over there and sit at your desk every day.

If you have carefully read this book and tried some of my suggestions, you can become one of the top 1% of the companies in your town. You will have the framework to expand beyond the borders of your town, and the limits of your imagination are only restricted by you. The first thing you need to do today is decide. Whether you have been in business for 30 years or less than 3 hours, you can learn something new and apply it right away.

Begin with a budget in mind and ask your accountant or bookkeeper to get the data to crunch the numbers and see where you're at. You might not like what you see, but at least you're going to face the information and know that you have a choice. You can decide to have a mediocre company with average results, or you can have a company that's legendary.

This statement might come across as very unusual, but it really is not about the money. Consider that two-thirds of the world's population lives on 2 dollars a day or less. Even if you are struggling, your biggest problem is somebody else's greatest dream, I promise you. It's really about what you become in the process and how you dispel any preconceived notions about who you are, your identity, and typecasting yourself. This experience has taught me to step out of my ego and comfort zone and appreciate all the subtleties that life lends us. Most of us aren't given a new lease on life, but I know I have and I wish the same for you.

The benefits of applying this knowledge or not, lie comfortably in your hands. If you believe you don't have enough time to take and apply the information in this book, then you're absolutely right. We are all only given one thing equally in this life, and that is 24 hours in a day. How you choose to spend those 24 hours is in your control. Our modern world is full of distractions that rob us of time. You know we can pick up extra minutes or hours every day, you don't need me here to tell you that. We both know we can avoid certain things, activities, social circles, and peer groups that perhaps are not serving our highest interest.

Take some time to sort through your priorities and figure out if where your life is now and how you want it to be, especially as it relates to your business. Are you willing to do the work to see and have a better future?

This might sound cliché, but with my minimum education, some college, and some technical training as well as some business school training I've been able to do this. I was hungry enough not just to get the information but to do something with it.

Toiling night and day to digest and comprehend information was important to me because I have a family and I want to provide for them. But this knowledge goes beyond me. It touches everybody that's in my sphere of influence. Applying this information and developing systems significantly influenced our team when I had my solar company. I looked at the multiplier effect of not just each employee, but each one of their family members and how one good deed truly pays it forward for others. Change the world, because the world needs you. Raise your standards and watch what's attracted to you. It works because I'm living proof that if I can do this, anyone can with enough hunger, drive, and passion.

I'm very proud of those moments and those times. I'd love to hear your story about how the shift occurred in you personally, as well as professionally. Visit our website at sunhedge.com and share with all of us what has changed in your life as a result of applying the information in this book.

# RESOURCES

This book is the tip of the iceberg and extrapolating all of the information into one book would prove to be challenging, as the book would be the size of an encyclopedia set.

This is why I felt it was not just important but necessary to provide you with access to some additional resources that allow you to dig deeper into the message of this book. My vision for you is to take this information and to read it, digest it, understand it, implement and improve it over time. So I've created a link that ties into the book, http://sunhedge.com/solarsuccessprinciples

**Caution**: These systems have been proven to be effective for those that take the information and apply it.
**Beware:** You will make more money, be happier, have an incredible culture at your company, and make customers into raving fans.

Life, as well as business will always be about implementation, so go get started. If you dismiss the ideas and goals in this book as not being right for you, could you envision a future where they would be? Head on over to our website, sunhedge.com and find the link for free resources. Check back often, there will be additional links on the website over time. My hope is to spread this education to the masses, raising the bar for small and large businesses and assisting you with your vision.

Made in the USA
Charleston, SC
25 August 2012